MUSIC OF THE EPHRATA CLOISTER.

PHOTO. BY J. F. SACHSE.

GENERAL VIEW OF THE KLOSTER GROUNDS AT EPHRATA.

The
Music of The Ephrata Cloister

ALSO

Conrad Beissel's Treatise on Music

AS SET FORTH IN A PREFACE TO THE

"Turtel Taube" of 1747

AMPLIFIED WITH FAC-SIMILE REPRODUCTIONS OF PARTS OF THE TEXT
AND SOME ORIGINAL EPHRATA MUSIC

OF THE

Weyrauchs Hügel, 1739; Rosen und Lilien, 1745; Turtel Taube,
1747; Choral Buch, 1754, etc.

BY

JULIUS FRIEDRICH SACHSE, Litt.D.

Member American Philosophical Society—Historical Society of Pennsylvania—Pennsylvania-German Society—American Historical Association—XIII International Congress of Orientalists, etc., etc.

Reprinted from Volume XII., Proceedings of the Pennsylvania-German Society

LANCASTER
PRINTED FOR THE AUTHOR
1903

AMS PRESS
NEW YORK

Reprinted from the edition of 1903, Lancaster, Pa.
First AMS EDITION published 1971
Manufactured in the United States of America

International Standard Book Number: 0-404-05500-1

Library of Congress Number: 77-134386

AMS PRESS INC.
NEW YORK, N. Y. 10003

PREFACE.

WIITHOUT doubt the music of the Ephrata Cloister, as evolved in the Settlement on the Cocalico, during the first half of the XVIII. century, and based on Beissel's peculiar system of harmony, exercised a far greater influence upon the community at large than is generally supposed. It not only had its effect upon the social life and development of the German settlers of Lancaster and adjoining counties who had fallen away from the orthodox faith of their fathers, by guiding their thoughts and minds into a spiritual channel; but it gradually extended its influence beyond its original bounds, across the Susquehanna; and in the course of a few years we find it installed in the valleys of the Antietam and Shenandoah where it found a lodgment until long after the parent community had passed out of existence.

It was even carried west of the Alleghanies, and into far-off New England, by these pious celibates, and it is not altogether improbable that one of the Ephrata tune books was largely instrumental in shaping the musical work of the Yankee tanner.

For many years this native Pennsylvania-German music

(3)

was a sealed book to the student and historian, but the recent discovery of the original score and tune books of the Cloister, together with Beissel's "Dissertation on Harmony," as set forth in the preface of the hymnal known as the *Turtel Taube*, enables us now for the first time to give the English reader a clear insight into this peculiar product. For the translation of the "Dissertation" and for the transposition of several musical numbers into modern notation, we are indebted to the Rev. J. F. Ohl, Mus.D., of Philadelphia.

Thanks are also due to General John F. Roller, of Harrisonberg, Va., for valuable aid rendered the writer in tracing the history of the German sectarians in Virginia; to Mr. W. H. Richardson, of Norristown, Pa., for two valuable illustrations; and to J. F. Mentzer, M.D., of Ephrata, and other fellow-members of the Pennsylvania-German Society who have so generously aided the writer in his researches during the past years.

JULIUS FRIEDRICH SACHSE.

PHILADELPHIA, December, 1902.

TABLE OF CONTENTS.

CHAPTER I.

THE MUSIC OF THE CLOISTER.

Unique Notation, Quaint Melodies — Earliest Ephrata Music — Contemporary Accounts, decline of the Community — Music Fostered at Snowhill Nunnery — Manuscript Music Books — Published Accounts — Beissel's Knowledge of Music — History of the Kloster — Dr. Wm. M. Fahnestock — Dr. Oswald Seidensticker — First Issue of the Ephrata Press — Title Pages — The Turtel Taube — Inadvertent Mistake — Score Book of the Cloister   6–23

CHAPTER II.

BEISSEL'S APOLOGY FOR SACRED SONG.

Scripture Texts — Song of the Godless — Song of the Early Christians — at the Table — Psaltery of Ten Strings — The Holy Spirit, the True Singing Master.   24–26

CHAPTER III.

THE MUSIC OF THE KLOSTER.

New Material — Correct Transposition, Beissel's System of Harmony — Ludwig Blum, Alleged Portrait — Curious Features of the Music — Movable C Clef — Seven-part Motet — Choral Songs, an Ephrata Sister   27–31

CHAPTER IV.

HYMN-BOOKS OF THE COMMUNITY.

Early Efforts at Hymnology — Franklin Imprints, Manuscript Hymnal — Wyrauchs Hügel — Song of the Solitary Turtel Taube — Wunderspiel — Rare and Interesting Titles — Great Hymnal — Sub-Titles — Various Editions — Prior Jaebez   32–52

CHAPTER V.

THE TURTEL TAUBE OF 1747.

Foreword — Original English Version — Power of the Church — Hymns and Music Adapted to Worship of God — Spirit of Singing, Mysteries of God — Conclusion of Foreword   53–58

CHAPTER VI.

FATHER FRIEDSAM'S DISSERTATION.

Facsimile of Prologue 59–65

CHAPTER VII.

Beissel's Unique Instructions on the Voice Relations of Pupil and Master — Demands of the Spirit — Kinds of Food — Effects of Milk, Cheese, Butter, Eggs, Honey — Cooked Dishes — Common Vegetables — Concerning Drink — Enochian Life 66–69

CHAPTER VIII.

BEISSEL'S DISSERTATION ON HARMONY.

Translator's Note — Qualification of Teacher — the Voices— What Constitutes a Four-part Tune — Barrir and Toener — Beissel's Explanation — Major and Minor Keys — Four-part Key for Melodies in C. — Key Diagram 70–79

CHAPTER IX.

ORIGINAL AND MODERN NOTATION.

Conclusion — Original Four-part Score on Single Staff — Rendition — Illustrations, Wohl auf in Four-part — Seven-part Motet — Five-part Melody — Six-part Choral — Rendition by Mrs. Frank Binnix — Sister Anna Thomen 80–92

APPENDIX.

A PAGE OF EPHRATA THEOSOPHY.

An Old Manuscript — German Proverb — Brother Obed — His Primer — A Newly-discovered Ephrata Imprint — Credit Due Pennsylvania-Germans — Appearance of Guardian Spirit — Various Transmigrations — Man's Cruelty — Woman's Frailty — Moral and Conclusions 93–106

LIST OF PLATES.

Negatives and Reproductions by JULIUS F. SACHSE.

The Ephrata Kloster, General View . . . . frontispiece
Portrait Late Professor Oswald Seidensticker . . . . . facing page 17
Specimen Page from Choral Buch . . . . "   "   40
Interior Views of Sister Saal or Chapel . . . . "   "   52
An Old Ephrata Hand Press . . . . "   "   96

ILLUSTRATIONS.

	PAGE.		PAGE.
Vignette, Wisdom	3	Peter Miller Portrait	51
Head Piece, Music	9	Head Piece, Cupid	53
Initial E	9	Script I	53
Snowhill Main Building	11	Tail Piece, Passion Cross	58
Ephrata Pen Work	12	Ephrata Water Mark	65
Ephrata Sampler	14	Head Piece, Lilies	66
Bethania	14	Vignette	66
Sister House and Chapel	15	Script Alphabet	69
Wm. M. Fahnestock	16	Head Piece, Beaux Art	70
Head Piece, Delicæ Ephraten-		Initial T	70
ses	24	Watermark, 1744	79
Ornate I	24	Head Piece and Initial	80
Tail Piece, "Laus Deo"	26	Tail Piece	86
Head Piece, Doves	27	Ephrata Symbol	92
Ephrata T	27	Seal Pennsylvania-German So-	
Silhouette Beissel	28	ciety	93
Ephrata Lily	31	Head Piece, Knowledge	95
Ephrata Sister	32	Vignette, Wisdom	95
Head Piece, Books and Pens	33	Schwenkfelder Inital	99
Ornate T	33	Tail Piece, "Finis"	106

TITLE PAGES AND MUSIC.

	PAGE.
Music, Earliest Ephrata, 1735 .	10
Arndt's Gebethe, Ephrata . .	17
Wunderschrift, Ephrata, 1745 .	18
Dissertatian on Man's fall, 1765 .	19
Chronicon Ephratense, 1786 . .	20
Leben eines Herzogs, Ephrata, 1790	21
Music, Gott ein Herscher . . .	30
Göttliche Liebes gethöne, 1730 .	34
Vorspiel der Neuen-welt, 1732 .	35
Paradisische Nachts Tropffen, 1734	36
Jacobs Kampf u. Ritter-Platz, 1736	37
Zionitischer Weyrauchs Hügel, 1739	38
Gesäng der Turtel Taube, 1747 .	39
Paradisisches Wunderspiel, 1754	40
Turtel Taube Nachklang, 1755 .	41
Turtel Taube Neuvermehrtes, 1762	41
Rosen u. Lilien. "Saron," 1756 .	42
Rosen u. Lilien. "Bethania," 1756	41
Wunderspiel, 1766	42
Ausbund geistreicher Lieder, 1785	43
Gilfende Hertzens-Bewegungen 1749	44
Turtel Taube, sub-titles . . .	46–48
Zionitischer Rosen Garten, 1754.	49

	PAGE.
Neuer Nachklang der Turtel Taube	52
Prologue, fac-simile	59–65
Barrir and Toener, fac-simile,	72
Music, four-part, key for Melodies in C, original and transposition	74
Music, Key Diagrams	76, 77
Music, original scores . . .	81
Music, Die Braut ist Erwachet (original)	82
Music, Die Braut ist Erwachet (modern)	83
Music, four-part anthem . . .	84
Music, Wie ist doch der Herr, five-part (original)	85
Music, Gott wir Kommen dir, five-part (original)	85
Music, Gedencke Herr an David, six-part (original) . . .	87
Music, Wohlauf und Schmücke, four-part (original) . . .	88
Music, four-part (modern) . . .	89
Music, Gott ein Herrscher aller Heiden 7-part Motet, Modern Notation	90, 91
Title, Ephrata Primer, 1786 . .	94
Title, Geistliche Briefe eines Friedsamen Pilgers Ephrata, 1794	98

CHAPTER I.

The Music of the Cloister.

VEN more interesting than the high-gabled cloister buildings at Ephrata, with their curious history and associations, or the issues of the printing office and writing room, with its ornate specimens of calig- raphy, is the music of the Ephrata Klo- ster, with its distinc- tive system of har- mony, unique nota- tion and quaint melodies, with a peculiar method of vocal rendition, all of which were an outgrowth of the the- osophy taught by Conrad Beissel and his followers on the Cocalico.

That this singular system of harmony (if strictly speak- ing it can be called a system), was an original evolution

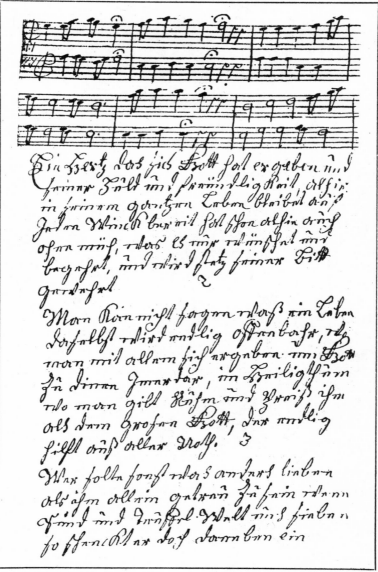

EARLIEST EPHRATA MUSIC—FROM MS. HYMN-BOOK USED AT AMWELL,
N. J., ABOUT 1735.

from the brain of the Magus on the Cocalico cannot be denied, and it has the additional distinction of being the first original treatise on harmony to be published in the western world. This was fully a quarter of a century before the Yankee tanner, William Billings, published his " New England Psalm Singer."

MAIN BUILDING OF THE SNOWHILL INSTITUTION.

Contemporary accounts by visitors to the Ephrata community during the eighteenth century, all bear witness to the peculiar sweetness and weird beauty of the song of the sisterhood, and the impressive cadence of the chorals and hymns of the combined choirs. Some writers even dwell upon the angelic or celestial quality of the vocal music as it floated through the spaces of the large Saal, as the responses were sung and reverberated from gallery to choir.

Much of the beauty of the music was no doubt due to the quality of the voices and the way they were used.

With the decline of the monastic or celibate feature of the Ephrata community, the music of the Kloster fell into disuse, and gradually became a lost art. The only place where any attempt was made to keep the Ephrata music alive, was at the institution known as the " Nunnery " at Snowhill in Franklin County. Here the music and Beis-

sel's system of harmony were fostered, taught and prac-
ticed until a few years ago, when the last of the Snowhill celibates passed from time into eternity.

SPECIMEN OF EPHRATA PENWORK FROM MS. HYMN-BOOK OF 1745.

It may truthfully be said that during the whole of
the nineteenth century no effort was made outside of the
Snowhill " Nunnery " to practice or keep alive this distinctive Pennsylvania-German music.

The manuscript music books, frequently embellished with beautiful penwork, became objects for the cupidity of the book collector, and are now scattered. A few have found resting-places in museums and great libraries of the country, but some of the best specimens are in private hands.

Unfortunately many of the music books of the Ephrata community deteriorated, by virtue of the peculiar composition of the ink used, which destroyed the fiber of the paper. Others again suffered from careless handling in addition to the ravages of time; then again in many cases copies were thrown aside or destroyed by their ignorant owners as worthless Dutch books. Thus it happens that the original collection of the Ephrata manuscript music, which was never a very large one, is now scattered, and specimens are eagerly sought after and difficult to obtain.

During the past quarter of a century the writer has made a systematic search for such music, scores and books, not passing even fragments. His search has been rewarded to so great an extent that it is now possible again to form a conception of Beissel's remarkable musical productions, and have them rendered once more in their original form.

Particular attention has also been devoted to the published accounts of Beissel's theories on harmony, in both the *Chronicon Ephratense* and the hymn-book known as the *Turtel Taube* of 1747. Comparisons have been made between original scores by Beissel and the elementary exercises used in the singing school, as well as with the finished and concerted pieces used at the Kloster services. Thus we are now in a position to form a tolerably clear idea of this system of harmony which had its development on the banks of the Cocalico, as well as of the original manner of rendering the music.

FROM AN EPHRATA SAMPLER.

Conrad Beissel evidently had but a scant acquaintance with the church music of the Reformation period, and his musical compositions, it now appears, stand in the same category with his theosophical writings. The music of the Ephrata Kloster is entirely unlike the ancient church music, and it has none of the rhythm and swing of either the religious or secular folk-song of the Reformation. Our

BETHANIA, THE OLD BROTHER HOUSE.

Ephrata music, like the hymns to which they were set, contains many elements of mysticism.

It will be remembered that this music, with its peculiar system of harmony, was a native Pennsylvania product—

the earliest and most original distinctive system of music evolved in the western world during the eighteenth century. Though crude in many of its progressions and often incorrect in its harmonies, yet from both an historical and a musical standpoint it is unique and valuable.

Sung as it was with fervor and feeling, by the enthusiastic mystic celibates within the confines of the Kloster Saal, the music unquestionably had a charm of its own.

The history of the old Kloster has for years been a fruitful subject for writers of varied accomplishments. No matter from what point of view we approach it — whether from a domestic, social, religious, educational or architectural one — we are astounded with the wealth of the novel situations which present themselves before us, changing at every turn with kaleidoscopic rapidity, ever presenting new

VIEW OF SAAL AND SARON.

SISTER HOUSE AND CHAPEL.

and curious combinations, and offering for consideration themes for study and an incentive for further research and discovery.

During the past quarter of a century, the reading public has been kept tolerably well informed of the history of this mystic community that had its origin in Lancaster County within our own State. In most cases these accounts were mere newspaper sketches, superficially written by the average reporter of the day, who usually has a vivid imagination, without any time or training for research or historic investigation.

DR. WM. M. FAHNESTOCK, b. APRIL 10, 1802; d. DEC. 15, 1854.

Even worse than these ephemeral stories, we have been afflicted with occasional dissertations and opinions by would-be authorities, who, although totally ignorant of the German tongue, and the habits and customs of our people and their literature, have set themselves up to speak authoritatively of the Ephrata people, their writings and

PROF. OSWALD SEIDENSTICKER,
B. MAY 3, 1825 ; D. JANUARY 10, 1894.

music. These, in almost every case have been mere idle vaporings, unworthy of notice and valueless for reference, except as to such portions as they have taken bodily from the publications of the Pennsylvania-German Society — or its members.

In bold contrast with the above screeds, we have a number of fugitive and fragmentary papers in both German and English — publications of great value by such writers, investigators and scholars as the late Dr. Wm. M. Fahnestock, Professor Oswald Seidensticker and others.

These publications were followed by the " Critical and Legendary History of the Ephrata Cloister and the Dunkers," an exhaustive work by the present writer, forming the basis of his "German Sectarians." This work, representing a research and labor of more than twenty years, was supposed to have been exhaustive, giving the whole history of the movement and settlement of the mystic community, as well as a complete list of the issues of the Ephrata press and a bibliography of the Kloster. But since its issue, a number of new imprints, broadsides and manuscripts have come to light, chiefly through the incentive offered by the pub-

TITLE OF ARNDT'S SPIRITUAL PRAYERS.

lished list in the "German Sectarians," among them being a copy of Arndt's *Gebethe*, supposed to have been the earliest issue of the Ephrata press.

So far as the writer has been able to discover in his investigations of the Ephrata press, there are evidences of

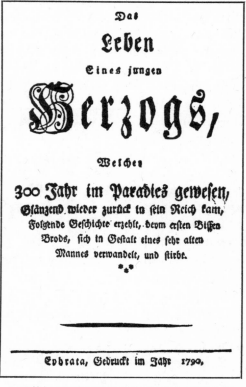

Das

Leben

Eines jungen

Herzogs,

Welcher

300 Jahr im Paradies gewesen,

Glänzend wieder zurück in sein Reich kam,
Folgende Geschichte erzehlt, beym ersten Bissen
Brods, sich in Gestalt eines sehr alten
Mannes verwandelt, und stirbt.

Ephrata, Gedruckt im Jahr 1790,

A LATELY DISCOVERED EPHRATA IMPRINT.

three instances where efforts were made to issue an original work of the community in both German and English.

The first of these was Beissel's *Wunderschrift* (1745). The English version, "A Dissertation on Man's Fall," was not printed until 1765.

Eine tiefe Angelegenheit meines Geistes hat mir Ursache gegeben diese Wunder-Schrifft aufzusetzen: u. etwas wehniges davon an den Tag zu geben, nemlich: durch welche unbeschreibliche Angelegenheiten ich daran gekommen bin. Und ob sich schon die Schrifft zur vollen Gnüge selbst anpreißt: so will doch, als zur Vorrede, etwas anmercken, um einen Eingang zur Sache zu machen.

Ich habe zwar in den Tagen meiner Göttlichen Jugend gemeinet, es könte mir nicht fehlen, wann ich mich würde auf das sauberste üben, um meinen Wandel im H. Verliebt-seyn und Göttlichen Lichte zu führen. Allein dieses hat so viel harte und schwere Gegensprüche erwecket, daß mich oft Entsetzen und Grausen ankam: wiewohl ich daneben mein H. Verliebt-seyn fortsetzte, in der Meinung es im Sieg zu gewinnen. Allein, je mehr Fleiß ich anwandt, desto eine hefftigere Rebellion ich in mir erweckte: welches mich freylich so geübet und gesiebet, daß oftmal die Steine, wann sie hätten eine Empfindlichkeit gehabt, mit mir hätten schreyen müssen, sonderlich weil der grose Fleiß und die allerreinste Brunst der Liebe allezeit das Feüer geschiert zu einem neuen Allarm. (1) Dieses hat mich freylich in gar

A

tiefes

(1) Der Sinn dieser Reden ist folgender: Je mehr wir uns lassen das Gute angelegen seyn, desto mehr wird das Uebel in uns rege. Es ist dieses eine aus langer Erfahrung bestätigte Warheit: dahero, wann wir

Gütes

INITIAL PAGE OF THE GERMAN VERSION OF BEISSEL'S WUNDERSCHRIFT.

A
Differtation on
MANS FALL,
Tranflated from the High-German Original.

DELICIAE EPHRATENSES

Printed: *EPHRATA* Anno MDCCLXV.
old at Philadelphia by Meffieurs CHRISTOPH
MARSHAL and WILLIAM DUNLAP

TITLE PAGE OF THE ENGLISH VERSION OF BEISSEL'S WUNDERSCHRIFT.

Chronicon Ephratenſe,

Enthaltend den Lebens-Lauf des ehrwürdigen Vaters in Chriſto

Friedſam Gottrecht,

Weyland Stiffters und Vorſtehers des geiſtl. Ordens der Einſamen tu
Ephrata in der Grafſchaft Lancaſter in PENNSYLVANIA.

Zuſamen getragen von Br. Lamech u. Agrippa.

Er iſt wie das Feuer eines Goldſchmieds, und wie die Seiffe der Wäſcher: Er
wird die Kinder Levi reinigen wie Gold und Silber. Malach. 3, 2. 3.

Es iſt die Zeit, daß anfahe das Gericht am Hauße Gottes, ſo aber zuerſt an
uns, was will vor ein Ende werden mit denen, die dem Evangelio Gottes
nicht glauben. Und ſo der Gerechte kümmerlich erhalten wird, wie will der
Gottloſe und Sünder erſcheinen 1. Petr. 4, 17.- 18.

EPHRATA: Gedruckt Anno M D C C L X X X V I.

TITLE PAGE OF CHRONICON EPHRATENSE.

The next venture was the *Chronicon Ephratense.* This
was translated by Brother Jaebez, and the MS. sent to
Christopher Marshall for correction and revision. The out-
break of the American Revolution prevented its publication.

The third work, and to us at present the most important
one, was Beissel's Dissertation on Harmony as it appears
in the preface of the *Turtel Taube* of 1747. The writer
has never been able to find a complete copy of this tractate in English. A fragment, however, has come down
to us, proving the fact that it was translated and printed
in English; but it unfortunately lacks the title and con-
cluding pages. Such portions as we have are printed
verbatim et literatim, the missing parts being translated
and supplied by the present writer.

The attention of the writer has been repeatedly called,
by musicians and other competent musical judges, to certain glaring errors in the music as printed in the musical
chapter of his work, and supposed to have been a correct
translation of the Ephrata scores into modern notation.
The writer greatly regrets the inadvertent introduction of
this erroneous matter into his work—mistakes for which
he can hardly be held responsible. In compiling the
chapter on the Ephrata music[1] the writer, not being an
expert skilled in the rules of harmony, nor proficient in
instrumental music, entrusted the transposition of several
specimen pieces into modern notation to the hands of a person whom he believed to be a competent and practical
musician — one who claimed to have some knowledge of
this kind of music. Fortunately for the writer, only three
of the transpositions were used.

The many criticisms which they brought forth led to a
closer and more general examination and study of such
Ephrata scores, manuscript music books and sheets as were

---

[1] "German Sectarians," Vol. II., Chapter VI., pp. 127-160.

available, and a comparison of them with such descriptive and explanatory matter as appears in the *Chronicon*, the *Turtel Taube* and other books of the Ephrata institution.

Since the issue of the final volume of the " German Sectarians," quite opportunely several new and heretofore unknown music books and manuscripts were found and brought forth from their resting-places, and were kindly sent, by their various inheritors, owners or legatees of some of the old Sabbatarians, to the writer. Two of these books deserve special mention, as they give to us the key to the whole system or manner of the rendition of the music, and how it was originally written or composed by the versatile genius on the Cocalico. These books, in fact, bear the same relation to Beissel's musical hieroglyphics that the Rosetta stone does to the Egyptian ones. One of these books appears to have been the score book of either Beissel or some other leader of the choirs. It also differs from any of the other known music books, as it contains some of the music as originally written by the composer, Conrad Beissel. In some places the entire four parts are written consecutively upon a single staff, the clef being shifted to suit the voice or part. In many cases the words of the hymns are also divided, showing the number of words sung respectively to each bar, which in many cases is an arbitrary selection.

The other book shows how the above four-part music, as originally written on a single staff, was written out when used in actual practice.

Another interesting bit of information that has come to light in this connection is " Beissel's Apology for Sacred Song," a colloquial tractate consisting of eleven questions and answers whereby Beissel justifies the introduction of sacred song. This tractate is now for the first time rendered into English and here follows.

CHAPTER II.

BEISSEL'S APOLOGY FOR SACRED SONG.

S it consistent with the Word of God that we sing?

Yes, as we find in both Old and New Testaments commands and examples. Psalm lxviii. 5, 33; Matthew xxvi. 30; Eph. v. 19; James v.13.

Who shall then sing?

All the saints of God, whose hearts and mouths are full of praise, thanksgiving and prayer.

Cannot the godless sing a hymn in a manner acceptable to God?

Oh, no, for, like unto the prayer of the wicked, so also is their song abhorrent unto God. The bawling of their hymns pleaseth Him not. Amos v.

Why cannot such people sing rightly?

Because they have not the spirit of Christ, who alone can intone the true tone and song.

How sang the early Christians?

One of the old chroniclers speaks thereof as follows :

"The husbandman sings behind the plow a joyful hallelujah; the tired reaper enlivens himself with psalms, and the vinedresser sings portions of David's hymns, and so forth."

At their meetings did they sing together?

Yes. For as they met together before break of day they read some selections, offered prayer, and in the simplicity of Christ sang hymns of praise as heathen writers have testified of them.

Did they sing at the table?

Yes. In place of disgraceful laughter and unnecessary conversation at the table, they, with wife, children and guests, intoned hymns of praise and thanksgiving.

How shall the heart be qualified when we want to sing?

As it has been crushed under the law and made pensive after God, then comes the Holy Ghost and brings peace and joy into the heart, that the mouth overflows to the praise of God.

What is meant by the psaltery with ten strings, of which David speaks?

As the tenth number is a perfect number (when one has counted ten, one begins again and commences with one), therefore is Christ our psaltery with ten strings, whose perfection is continually in our hearts and to be sung with our lips.

Who therefore teaches us to sing aright?

The Holy Spirit, as the true singing-master, can turn the heart into a celestial harp and divine instrument, so that it can be used without outward instrument and sound, and often also without any audible voice.

Is it not sufficient when one outwardly listens to a beautiful melody?

Oh, no.   Paul speaks: " Sing unto the Lord in or with your hearts."   Even the lips of the godless can carry a fine voice.

Intone then ye saints to the Lord, intone a hymn unto the Lord, with the celestial choirs of the upper and lower Jerusalem; yea, let everything that hath breath praise the Lord.

Hallelujah.

CHAPTER III.

The Music of the Kloster.

HE finding of this new material and the discovery of other interesting features of mystical Pennsylvania music, together with an earnest desire of the writer to correct the evident errors in the musical transcriptions in his chapter on the Ephrata music, have been among the incentives to write this paper, and thereby to perfect his account of the Kloster music. For this purpose he has secured the coöperation of the Rev. J. F. Ohl, Mus. Doc., well known as a musical editor and writer on musical subjects. This authority has made correct transpositions of the native Pennsylvania-German music into modern notation, enabling us to present in its proper light the peculiar system of harmony evolved in the versatile brain of Conrad Beissel in his seclusion on the Cocalico. A number of illustrations, sufficient for our purpose, are given both in the original and in modern form.

The system of harmony here brought to our notice, it must be remembered, was the original outgrowth of the

(27)

mind of a comparatively uneducated man, whose practical knowledge of music was limited to a few scrapings of dance music when he was yet a journeyman baker in the Fatherland.   How much instruction he may have received in theoretical or practical notation from Ludwig Blum during the latter's short sojourn on the Cocalico it is difficult to surmise.   But, judging from the tenor of the Ephrata

ALLEGED PORTRAIT OF CONRAD BEISSEL.

records, Beissel evidently received no information from Blum, except such as was carried to him by Sister Anastasia and her associates.   Yet here we find Conrad Beissel, we may say almost at a moment's notice, without previous preparation, teaching and publishing novel rules on harmony, composition and vocal music — taking for his guide, the records inform us, the Æolian harp — in other words, the music of nature ; and in less than twenty years he composes, it is stated, over a thousand different melodies and tunes, set in two, four, five, six and even seven parts, to as many different hymns, most of which were also of his composition.

A curious feature of this Ephrata music is that it was chiefly sung by female voices ; thus the four-part pieces were rendered by a female tenor, alto and soprano, the music being written in the movable C clef, while the bass appears in the F clef. In the five-part scores, a second bass is added, making three female and two male parts. The six-part compositions have the same arrangement, with the addition of another female tenor. An additional high female voice completes the seven-part music, which I believe stands unique in musical literature. This had five female parts and two male : viz., two sopranos or high female voices, one alto or counter tenor, two female tenors, and first and second bass.

The peculiar arrangement of the voices prevailed in all the Ephrata music, a peculiarity which is distinctly mentioned in different contemporary MSS., which state that all the parts save the bass, which is set in two parts, are led and sung exclusively by the females. Thus, in the seven-part music, counting from below, the first part is lower bass ; second, upper bass ; third, female tenor ; fourth, female treble ; fifth, counter, high female voice ; sixth, leading voice ; seventh, second leading voice.

Our illustration of Beissel's seven-part music, *Gott der Herscher aller Heiden*, is taken from the *Paradisisches Wunderspiel* of 1754, which was his last musical work,

GOTT ein Herrscher aller Heyden, der sein Volck bald wird herrlich leiten,
und ihr Recht lassen hoch hergehn: wenn ER Zion schön wird
schmücken, ihr Heil wird lassen näher rücken, so wird man Freud und Wonne sehn

an Seinem Eigenthum, das nun giebt Preiß und Ruhm GOTT dein König,
der sie erhöht, ihr Völcker seht! wie GOttes Braut nun einhergeht. 196.

A SEVEN-PART MOTET.

and the *Chronicon* says that it was by many masters declared the most important. These were the choral songs, and they consist of a folio volume partly written, partly printed.

AN EPHRATA SISTER FROM ILLUMINATED HYMN-BOOK.

CHAPTER IV.

The Hymn-Books of the Community.

THE earliest hymn and music books of the Ephrata community were all laboriously and carefully executed with the pen. These were supplanted by the hymn-books printed for their use by Franklin in 1730, 1732 and 1736, and Sauer in 1739. Shortly after the large printing press was established in the institution on the Cocalico the membership as well as the number of original hymns and tunes having greatly increased, it was proposed to issue a distinctive original hymn-book for the uses of both the solitary and secular organizations, all of the compositions being the work of the inmates of the Kloster and set to tunes of their own. This book was to replace in the Kloster worship those previously printed by Franklin as well as the *Weyrauchs Hügel*, which bears the imprint of Christopher Sauer of Germantown.

GOTTLICHE

Liebes und Lobes gethöne

Welche in den hertzen der kinder
der weiſzheit zuſammen ein.

Und von da wieder auſzgefloſſen

ZUM LOB GOTTES,

Und nun denen ſchülern der himliſchen
weiſzheit zur erweckung und auf-
munterung in ihrem Creutz und
leiden aus hertzlicher liebe mitgetheilet.

DANN

Mit lieb erfüllet ſein, bringt Gott den beſten Preiſs
Und giebt zum ſingen uns, die allerſchönſte weiſz.

Zu *Philadelphia:* Gedruckt bey *Benjamin*
Franklin in der *March-ſtraſs.* 1730,

HYMNALS OF THE EPHRATA COMMUNITY.

VORSPIEL
DER
NEUEN-WELT.

Welches sich in der letzten Abendroethe
als ein paradisischer Lichtes-glantz
unter den Kindern Gottes
hervor gethan.

IN

LIEBES, LOBES, LEIDENS, KRAFFT
und Erfahrungs liedern abgebildet, die
gedrückte, gebückte und Creutz-
tragende Kirche auf Erden.

Und wie inzwischen sich

Die obere und Triumphirende Kirche
als eine Paradiesische vorkost hervor thut und offenbahret.

Und daneben, als

Ernstliche und zuruffende wächterstimmen
an alle annoch zerstreuete Kinder Gottes, das sie
sich sammlen und bereit machen auf den
baldigen ; Ja bald herein brechen-
den Hochzeit-Tag der braut
des Lämms.

Zu *Philadelphia* : Gedruckt bey *Benjamin*
Francklin, in der *Marck-strass.* 1732.

Paradiesische Nachts Tropffen
Die Sich in der Stille zu Zion als
ein lieblicher morgen tau
über die Kinder Gottes
aus gebreitet.

und

In Sonderheit

Denen zu den Füssen Jesu Sitzenden Kindern
Ihrer inwendigen erweckung und
wahren hertzens andacht

als

Eine rechte und Göttliche Schulübung um
die wahre und geheime Ja im
Geist hier verborgen
liegende
Sing-Kunst zu lernen.

mitgetheilet
und

ans Licht gegeben

Im Jahr 1 7 3 4

HYMNALS OF THE EPHRATA COMMUNITY.

JACOBS
Kampff- und Ritter-Platz

ALLWO

Der nach feinem urfprung fich fehnende
geift der in Sophiam verliebten feele
mit Gott um den neuen namen
gerungen, und den Sieg
davon getragen.

ENTWORFFEN

IN UNTERSCHIDLICHEN GLAUBENS-
u. leidens-liedern, u. erfahrungs vollen aus-
truckungen des gemuths, darinnen fich
dar ftellet, fo wol auff feiten Gottes
feine unermuedete arbeit zur rei-
nigung folcher feelen, die fich
feiner fuerung anvertraut.

ALS AUCH

Auff feiten des Menfchen der ernft des
geiftes im aus halten unter dem procefs
der läuterung und abfchmeltzung
des Menfchen der Sünden famt
dem daraus entfpringen-
den lobes-gethön.

ZUR

Gemüthlichen erweckung derer die das heil
Jerufalems lieb haben.

VERLEGET

Von einem liebhaber der wahrheit die im ver-
borgenen wohnt.

Zu *Philadelphia,* gedruckt bey B. F. 1736.

ZIONITISCHER

Weyrauchs Hügel

Oder:

Myrrhen Berg,

Worinnen allerley liebliches und wohl riechen=
des nach Apotheker = Kunst zu bereitetes
Rauch = Werck zu finden.

Bestehend

In allerley Liebes = Würckungen der in GOTT
geheiligten Seelen, welche sich in vieler und mancherley
geistlichen und lieblichen Liedern aus gebildet.

Als darinnen

Der letzte Ruff zu dem Abendmahl des gros=
sen GOttes auf unterschiedliche Weise
trefflich aus gedrucket ist;

Zum Dienst

Der in dem Abend = Ländischen Welt = Theil als
bey dem Untergang der Sonnen erweckten Kirche
GOttes, und zu ihrer Ermunterung auf die
Mitternächtige Zukunft des Bräutigams
ans Licht gegeben.

Germantown ; Gedruckt bey Christoph Sauer. 1739

HYMNALS OF THE EPHRATA COMMUNITY.

Das
Gesäng
Der einsamen und verlassenen
Turtel-Taube
Nemlich der Christlichen
Kirche.

Oder geistliche u. Erfahrungs-volle Leidens u. Liebes-Gethöne,
Als darinnen beydes die Vorkost der neuen Welt als
auch die darzwischen vorkommende Creutzes-und Leidens-
Wege nach ihrer Würde dargestellt, und in
geistliche Reimen gebracht

Von einem Friedsamen und nach der
stillen Ewigkeit wallenden

Pilger.

Und nun
Zum Gebrauch der Einsamen und Verlassenen zu Zion
gesammlet und ans Licht gegeben

EPHRATA.
Drucks der Brüderschafft im Jahr 1747.

HYMNALS OF THE EPHRATA COMMUNITY.

Paradisisches
Wunder-Spiel,
Welches sich
In diesen letzten Zeiten und Tagen
In benen Abend-Ländischen Welt-Theilen als ein Vor-
spiel der neuen Welt hervor gethan. Bestehende
In einer gantz neuen und ungemeinen Sing-
Art auf Weise der Englischen und himm-
lischen Chören eingerichtet.

Da dann das Lied Mosis und des Lamms, wie auch das hohe Lied Salomo-
nis samt noch mehrern Zeugnüssen aus der Bibel und andern Heiligen
in liebliche Melodyen gebracht. Wobey nicht weniger der Zuruf der
Braut des Lamms, samnt der Zubereitung auf den herzlichen
Hochzeit-Tag trefflich Præfigurirt wird.

Alles nach Englischen Chören Gesangs-Weise mit viel Mühe und großem Fleiß
ausgefertiget von einem

Friedsamen,
Der sonst in dieser Welt weder Namen noch Titul suchet.

EPHRATÆ Sumptibus Societatis: 1 7 5 4 ;

TITLE PAGE OF BEISSEL'S MOST IMPORTANT MUSICAL WORK,
THE FOLIO CHORAL BOOK.

SPECIMEN PAGE FROM CHORAL BOOK. THE NOTES AND EMBELLISHMENTS ARE ALL PEN WORK. A COMBINATION OF TYPE, PEN AND ARTISTIC COLOR WORK.

Nachklang
Zum
Gesäng der einsamen

Turtel Taube,

Enthaltend eine neue Sammlung Geistlicher Lieder.

EPHRATA Drucks der Brüderschafft
Im Jahr 1 7 5 5 .

Neuherausgehrtes
Gesäng der einsamen
Turtel-Taube,

Zur gemeinschafftlichen Erbauung gesammlet und ans Licht gegeben.

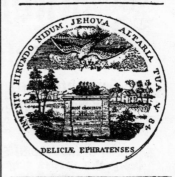

EPHRATÆ Typis Societatis Anno 1 7 6 2 .

Ein
Angenehmer Geruch der

Rosen und Lilien

Die im Thal der Demuth unter den Dornen hervor gewachsen.

Alles aus der Schwesterlichen Gesell-
schafft in SARON.

Im Jahr des Heils 1 7 5 6 .

Ein
Angenehmer Geruch der

Rosen und Lilien

Die im Thal der Demuth unter den Dornen hervor gewachsen.

Alles aus der Brüderlichen Gesell-
schafft in BETHANIA.

Im Jahr des Heils 1 7 5 6 .

LATER ADDITIONS TO THE TURTEL TAUBE OF 1747.

Paradiſiſches

Wunder-Spiel,

Welches ſich

In dieſen letzten Zeiten und Tagen in denen Abend-
ländiſchen Welt-Theilen, als ein Vorſpiel
der neuen Welt hervorgethan:

Beſtehend in einer neuen Sammlung andächtiger und zum Lob
des groſen Gottes eingerichteter geiſtlicher, und ehedeſſen
zum Theil publicirter Lieder.

EPHRATÆ: Typis & Conſenſu Societatis A: D: M D C C L X V I.

THE GREAT HYMNAL OF THE EPHRATA COMMUNITY.

Außbund

Geiſtreicher Lieder.

Ephrata, Gedruckt im Jahr 1785.

TITLE PAGE OF LAST HYMN-BOOK PRINTED BY THE EPHRATA COMMUNITY.
(Original in collection of the writer.)

Gilfende

Herßenß-Bewegungen

Der unter die Fittigen der verlaſſenen Turtel-Taube geſammleten

Einſamen.

Welche das Wunder der himmliſchen Weisheit in eine geiſt-
liche Schule zuſammen gebracht: in welcher ſie in mancherley geiſtlichen Uebungen den Wittwen-und
Wayſen-Stand erlanget.

Und ſolchen in geiſtlichen Andachten und Liedern an Tag gezeen.
Welche nun, zur gemeinſchafftlichen Erbauung, als ein Nach-
klang dem Geſäng der verlaſſenen Turtel-
Taube angehänget ſind.

EPHRATA in Penſylvanien
Drucks und Verlags der Brüderſchafft. Anno MDCCXLIX.

SUB-TITLE OF THE EPHRATA TURTEL TAUBE.

Der
Geistliche Braut-Schmuck
Der heiligen
Jungfrauen = und Glieder-Zahl
Des
Lamms.

Das
KIRREN
Der einsamen und verlassenen
Turtel-Tauben.

Die Chöre des Himmels stimmen mit an, und die
Geister, die vor GOTT stehen, schallen mit hernieder.

Die
Braut des Lamms,
als sie erwecket wird
Durch die Stimme ihres Geliebten, übersteiget.
im Prophetischen Geist
die
Myrrhen-Berge,
und erblicket ihre zukünfftige Verweilung
unter
Rosen und Lilien.

This movement resulted in the issue in 1747 of a small quarto of 360 pages, seven and one half inches by six inches, known as the *Turtel Taube*, which contains some 277 hymns. This book, so far as we know, was the first original hymn-book printed at Ephrata, and the first to be printed in the western world, wherein all of the hymns were original compositions.

This collection is divided into six parts, viz:

(1) *Der geistliche Brautschmuck der heiligen Jungfrauen*, 60 hymns.

(2) *Das Kirren der Einsamen und Verlassenen Turteltauben*, 62 hymns.

(3) *Die Braut des Lamms, als sie erwecket wird*, anthem and choral.

(4) *Abend-ländische Morgen-Röthe*, 88 hymns.

(5) *Gilfende Hertzens-Bewegungen*, 35 hymns.

(6) No special title, but ornamental head piece, 31 hymns.

Nun folget die
Abend-ländische Morgen-Röthe,
die sich am Abend der Zeiten ausgebreitet
über die Christliche

Kirche,
Darinnen beydes der bald heran-brechende Tag ihrer Erlösung,
als auch ihre nächtliche Verweilung unter
dem Creutz erblicket wird:
vorgestelt in geistlichen
Gesängen.

About two-thirds of these hymns were contributed by
Conrad Beissel. The collection of hymns, 277 in number,
is prefaced by a foreword of five pages, and a prologue of
fourteen pages, the whole really forming, as before stated,
a treatise on harmony. At the end of the volume there
is an epilogue and conclusion of " the song of the solitary
and deserted turtle dove," an invocation of three pages in
bold display type, followed by the usual index.

Two other editions of the Turtel Taube of 1747 were
issued subsequently without change of date, but differing

Von der
Zerfallenen Hütte
Davids,
Und ihrer Wiederaufrichtung
Durch den, der da ist das Panier der
Völcker.
Aus der Prophetischen Wurzel aufgesucht/ und zur
Kirchlichen Uebung mitgetheilet von einem
nach der stillen Ewigkeit wallenden
Friedsamen.

somewhat in the arrangement after page 294, together
with the addition of a large number of hymns, and an
elimination of a few of the original edition. Thus, in the
second edition 1749 the part known as the *Gilfende Hertzens-Bewegungen* consists of 114 hymns all of which are
the work of the solitary brothers and sisters. Most of the
hymns of the sixth part of the original edition are rele-

gated to the fifth part, and an entire new part containing
47 hymns by Beissel is added under the title " *Von der
Zerfallenen Hütte Davids, und ihrer Wiederaufrichtung,*"
etc. The collation of this edition is the same as above

**Ein
Geiſtliches Denckmahl und Lobſpruch**
Aufgerichtet
Zur Befrönnng des Prieſter Ordens der Einſamen in
EPHRATA,
Von einer Streiterin JEſu Chriſti,
Welche viele Jahre im geiſtlichen Marterthum
zugebracht.

---

except that it contains 372 hymns, pp. 495; no epilogue
but seven pages of index.

The last and complete edition of the *Turtel Taube* of
1747, issued during the next decade without change of

Nachrede.
**Der Geiſt ſchlieſet mit einem Freuden=
reichen Lob und Danck, und einem
Prophetiſchen Geruch der Lilien.**

---

date, is virtually the same as the one just described except
that a page of hymns is added in brevier. Then follows:

" A spiritual monument and Eulogy Erected for the
crowning of the priestly order of the solitary in EPH-

RATA, by a female Warrior of Jesus Christ who for
many years has suffered spiritual Martyrdom;" this is followed by an epilogue,

"The spirit closes with an abundance of Praise and
gratitude, and a prophetic fragrancy of Lilies," the last
page of this epilogue being the same as the one in the
original edition, except that it is printed in the regular
type. The additional matter forms eight pages and the
usual index is also included in the book. It is in the prologue of this hymn-book that our interest centers at the
present time, as it contains Conrad Beissel's dissertation
on harmony, setting forth his peculiar system of music.
As has been previously stated there was an English version of both foreword and prologue. A fragment, however, of the former alone is known to the present writer.

A complete translation of the foreword is here presented, such parts of the original English version being
presented verbatim. The whole matter as now given in
its entirety, amplified by fac-similes of original scores, text
and Beissel's apology for the introduction of sacred song
into the curriculum of the Kloster, will enable the student of
the future to form a better conception of this peculiar outgrowth of the mystical Kloster theosophy on the Cocalico
than was heretofore possible, while to the would-be critic,
who is non-conversant with the German tongue and the
history of the mystical speculations of the Ephrata Community, it will offer an insight into Conrad Beissel's strictly
Pennsylvania-German musical structure.

Before passing too strict a judgment on this music for
its constant violation of the accepted rules of harmony, let
us consider how both hymns and music originated.

These hymns and tunes were virtually the outpourings
of religious enthusiasts, whose nervous systems had been
wrought up to a high pitch by incessant vigils, fast-

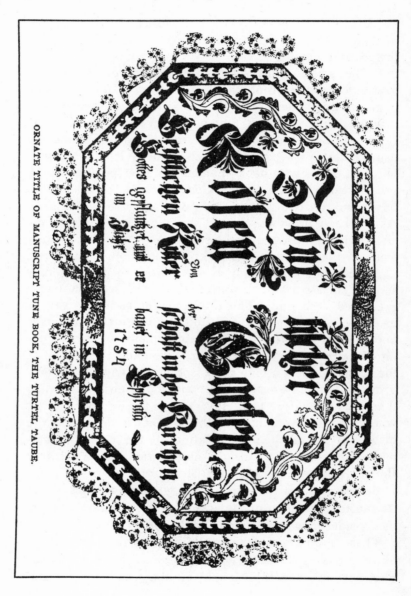

ings and an abstemious mode of life. Then, again, it must be considered that neither Beissel nor his musical co-laborers seemed to understand anything about harmony beyond the rules governing the common chord and its inversions. So far as known no one connected with the community was a skilled musician.

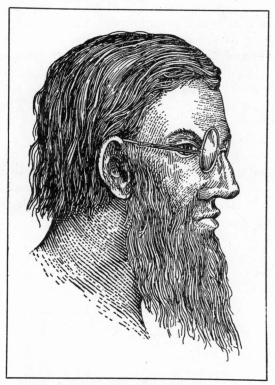

THE ONLY KNOWN PORTRAIT OF PRIOR JAEBEZ
(REV. JOHN PETER MILLER).

Just who the author was of the foreword and prologue cannot be definitely stated; it is usually credited wholly to Beissel. The dissertation on harmony is undoubtedly

solely his own composition. The literary portion, however, shows the evident pruning of Prior Jaebez (Rev.
Peter Miller) who was without question the translator of
the original English version.

A page of the most important part of the system of harmony is reproduced in fac-simile the better to enable the
reader who does not have access to an original copy to
compare the present translation with the original.

The utility of presenting a complete translation of this
matter prefixed to the *Turtel Taube* may be questioned
by some. In the writer's chapter on the Ephrata music
in his *German Sectarians*, only the vital parts bearing on
Beissel's system of harmony were presented. The desire
having been expressed in some quarters that it were well
to have the matter in its entirety, regardless of its mystical
and vague phraseology, the whole matter is here presented,
together with fac-similes of the subtitles, and illustrations
of the "Spiritual Monument" and Epilogue, which are to
be found in only a very few of the known specimens of
the *Turtel Taube* of 1747.

Neuer Nachklang des Gesängs der einsamen Turtel Taube.

A Ey GOtt! sieh doch ein-
mal auf meinen grosen
Schmerzen, u. wie der Kum-
mer mir das Leben saugt und
nagt: ich hab ja allen Fleiß u.
Treu von gantzem Hertzen, da-
zu mein Leben selbst, aufs äu-
ferst hin gewagt: kanst du dañ
sehen zu? ich muß ja fast ver-
gehen von grosem Hertzenleid,
weil du nicht hörst mein Flehen

2. Warum bist du so hart
dem armen Thon und Leimen?
ich bin ja nicht ein Fels, der
solches tragen kan; wilt mich
dann deine Güt im Hertzenleid
aufräumen, daß muß seyn wie
verirrt auf deiner Lebens-Bahn
ich habe ja um dich mein Alles
hingeben, und hab doch allmein
Tag ein kümerliches Leben.

3. Ist dann vergessen gar

wie deine grose Güte mich hat
so väterlich gerissen aus der
Welt, da ich vor vielem Leid
offt war von Seufzen müde,
um also nur allein zu thun, was
dir gefällt. Wie freudig konte ich bald alles fahren lassen,
weil sich dein grose Güt so häuf-
fig sehen lassen.

4. U. ob es gleichwohl scheint,
als wäre ich vergessen, so hör
ich doch nicht auf zu stehen deine Treu; und ob schon manchen
Tag und Jahr betrübt geses-
sen, so weiß ich doch, mein
GOtt wird mir noch stehen bey.
Obgleich der Jammer groß in
den betrübten Tagen, so werde
ich doch noch von Gottes Güte sagen.

5. Doch ist annoch zur Zeit
derselbe Trost verborgen, weil

HYMNALS OF THE EPHRATA COMMUNITY.

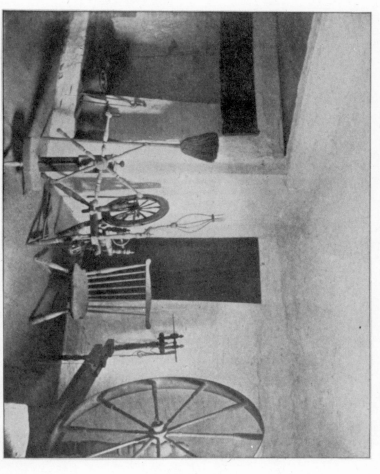

A COMMUNITY ROOM IN THE SISTER HOUSE AT EPHRATA.

CHAPTER V.

THE TURTEL TAUBE OF 1747.[2] FOREWORD.

T IS written, "Behold a Tabernacle of God With men." Rev 21. There is a dam broken of the heavenly ocean, through the forthcoming of the Church. Which from eternal ages remained concealed in God, as between Father and Son: but in due time appeared among men, and has now as in the last days, shown forth herself anew, with vigor and strength as in the early ages.

This holy Church, having through the heavenly dove; which in the early days decended upon our high head Christ, at his baptism; appeared in the world, and from time to time drawn souls unto herself, who under her protection, remained steadfast unto the end in their calling, we believe the Church to possess, a renewing, reviving, and sanctifying power. And that all, spoken of by the prophets and apostles, which should come to pass in future ages, finds its beginning in the Church; in which all the wonders and powers of future glory are found concealed. Whosoever therefore, honoreth the Church, honoreth God: for God is in the Church; and he that abideth in the Church, abideth in God, and has his free city, where he

---

[2] Original English version.

may find protection when pursued by the blood-avenger of the powers of darkness.　Deut. 19.

After the same manner in which God, reveals forward into eternity through the Church, all his mysteries : it also remains for him to receive from the Church, praise, and the glorifying of his name, unto everlasting ages.　In accordance with this, it was ordained by the spirit of the Church, or heavenly dove, that the talent of singing should be added unto spiritual services, and be employed in outspreading the praise of God unto endless ages.

By the use of this talent the holy angels, made known the near approach of the Church, when they at the incarnation of him, who was the heart of the Church; entered within her borders, and by singing gave honor unto his appearance in the flesh.

We who were lying at the hedges, having by the goodness of God, been brought unto the Church, that we might become heirs to the kingdom prepared for the righteous, through the sanctification of the blood of Christ, he, who is the heart of the CHURCH.　We have in this Church found a strong support in setting forward our spiritual labors ; and greatly find ourselves indebted unto her for the many privileges bestowed upon us, from which we have derived so much profit.　For untill the present, she has been unto us, when forsaken, our spiritual mother; when comfortless, our nurse; in cold, our garment; in heat, our shadow; in shame, our crown; in loss, our gain; and in want, our abundance : yea, she has outspread herself over us, with her wings, like a hen over her little ones, and protected us from the robbing hawks of the regions of despair.

We nevertheless found, upon entering into the Church, a contrariness of things, between ourselves and the spirit,

preparing the way to a newness of life. For as said before, God having ordained, that through the church his
name should be glorified; there were required, voices,
hymns and music written for the use of the singers.

After the manner of heavenly things, there was found in
the Church an outflowing fountain of good. On the contrary, our state of being brought this with itself that the
good which flowed from the Church, was continually con-
sumed by our selfishness: through which such a loss might
have fallen upon the Church, as would have exhausted the
original fountain of good; had there not remained in the
mystery of the Church, causes, through which her losses
could be restored.

Now as such a selection of hymns and music adapted to
the worship of God; was not to be sought in our own
abilities, nor in the power of the unsanctified mind: (for
by the unsanctified mind, heaven is constantly being locked
up,) but in the abilities which God bestows: so we found
it necessary constantly to renew our diligence in practicing
selfdenial, if at all heaven should again be unlocked at our
natural state, and the praise of God from thence brought
out. So much then, as we made it our object to gain a
knowledge of church music, and to improve the talent of
singing; so much was the toil and labor to be overcome.

In this way we were brought to see the loftiness of
heavenly things, the little value of our own works, and at
the same time were placed in a state of poorness of spirit
wherein alone the highway of holiness is found. Isa 55.
For the Church does not allow us to suppose that we of
ourselves can accomplish any good; and he that has with
all his works become subject unto the Church; the same
has indeed attained a deep state of spiritual poverty.

On the contrary, so far as consolation is sought in the

amusements of the visible world, so far we lose communion with the Church: the spirit of singing, as the heavenly dove, retreats: and the praise of God is no more heard. It is therefore of the greatest importance to be always engaged in laboring for the prosperity of the church; and it cannot well be expressed in few words, what attention must be paid to a careful walk of life, and what acquirements are necessary, to establish excellent church music.

In this course of life, there is learned, the constant coming off from one's self; which is by all means necessary, if an agreement of understanding, and a unity of spirit is to be brought forth and established in our midst. Therefore, as all this is found in the Church, we may expect; that therein trials without any cessation will continue to arise; through which our human nature may be so far subdued as to allow the praise of God constantly to flow from the heart.

We also have in the Church, a sure prospect, with respect to the salvation, which shall in due time, be revealed unto all those who did not flee at the approach of trials, but have sought to remain faithful in the service of their divine Master. Here it nevertheless at length followed, after we had long silent remained, that our spirits aroused under the pressure, and coming to a state of heavenly meditation gave God the glory who called us to such a work which far exceeds anything which the natural mind is able to comprehend. We therefore feel inclined to bestow the highest praise upon the Church, for having brought us under her control and government that we without her consent, are not allowed to determine upon some particular course of our own. Which, in like manner as it brought trials upon human nature it also had the tendency to bring to light an abundant supply of hymns, and that for the most part in those directions where the ice was first broken.

In a general sense, the hymns contained in this selection, may be looked upon as roses which have grown forth from among the piercing thorns of the cross, and consequently are not without some beauty of color and pleasantness of fragrance.

And so far as the greater portion of them is concerned, were brought to light in the rigid school of the cross, within a period of many years, and for the most part by persons who labored much for the edification of the Church.

The spirit of the Church, having taught us in the course of our spiritual labors, to place a high estimation upon the hymns of the followers of Christ, brought forth in their trials under the cross; and believing them to be instructive, we have concluded to secure them as treasures, and have in the compilation as well as in the print of this work, applied our utmost care that no errors might occur through which occasion might be taken to give our labors a low estimation.

But to speak yet further of the compilation of this spiritual work; it is a field of flowers, grown forth of many different colors, and of various fragrance : as they were produced by the spirit of the Church, out of the *Mysterio* of God. In some the spirit of prophecy, soared above all mountains of the cross; bidding defiance to his enemies; setting forth as present, the future glory of the Church. In others, the spirit trod into the inner court, and exalted his voice in the holiest of all. Again, others, have the pleasant odor of roses; others, on the contrary, sprung up upon the myrrh mountains.

[Here ends the fragment of the original English version in my possession, J. F. S.]

[Now as the Church hath extended herself, so also have the voices increased in our own spiritual school, in which our hearts were the praise of the great God. And any one who has had only a limited experience in this, our spiritual school, can readily perceive that in this entire work can be found naught that reminds one of human effort or wild fancy, but that the words of the spiritual songs herein contained, sprang from many and varied emotions.

Here we would conclude our foreword, did not an important matter still remain. For after having come into possession of so rich a treasure for the praise of God, it became a question in our spiritual school how our voices could be cultivated for spiritual song; hence such a matter of spiritual practice became imperatively necessary as would bring the voices into spiritual harmony and at the same time make our sacrifice of praise conformable to good common sense. Therefore we will now impart the preliminary treatise on singing, which we esteem necessary to give completeness to the work.]

[As the first part of the German Prologue does not bear directly on the subject under discussion, we give this only in *facsimile.*]

CHAPTER VI.

Eine
Sehr deutliche
Beschreibung,
Wie sich das hohe und wichtige
Werck unserer geistlichen
Sing-Arbeit
Erboren, und was der Nutzen von der
Gantzen Sach sey.
Gegeben
Von einem Friedsamen und nach
Der stillen Ewigkeit wallenden Pilger.

ES wird durch diese kleine Beschreibung ein Bericht ertheilet von einem nicht geringen Preiß beydes der Weißheit und Güte unsers Gottes, wie nemlich selbe uns entsiegelt das Geheimnus des Creuzzes, wodurch das in GOtt verlohrne Gut wieder gefunden, da die ewige Weißheit des Vatters als der Sohn Gottes seinen Trohn-Sitz verlassen, und aus seiner Kammer zu uns heraus in diese Welt ging, und die Bottschafft des Friedens an uns gebracht, und die Erlösung durch sich selbst am Creutz entsiegelt und offenbaret, und nach ausgeführtem Process, wiederum zum Vatter gekehret, und in seine Kammer eingegangen, und sein beruffnes Volck, Kirche, oder Gemeine, mit derselbigen Hoffnung und Vertröstung das Er wieder kemmen, und sein sich nehmen wolle (Schaar) in dieser streitbaren Welt gelassen) dabey

Vorrede über die Sing-Arbeit.

dabey den Göttlichen Brief der Bottschafft des Friedens mit dem Siegel des Creutzes, Leidens u. Sterbens in ihren Händen gelassen, mit dem Befehl, solche Bottschafft aus zu tragen biß an die Ende der Erden, doch so, daß sie solten warten, biß sie angethan würden mit Krafft aus der Höhe, welches alles erfüllet u. geschehen, daß der Aufgang aus der Höhe von da an sich über die gantze Erde ausgebreitet, und die Bottschafft des Friedens mit GOtt fast allen Völckern kund worden, samt dem Geheimniß des Creutzes, worauf der Friedens-Contract beruhete. Dahero es auch auf eine gar wunderbare Weiß bald an ein seltsames Würgen und Schlachten ging, zu welcher Zeit sich der Saame von dem Wort des Lebens und des Creutzes gesäet, auch fortgewachsen und bis auf uns kommen. Und weilen er gar nachdrücklich mit derselbigen Hoffnung verknüpfft: so hat sichs auch zugetragen, daß wir neben denen mühsamen Creutzes- und Leidens-Ständen, womit wir beladen, als das Wort des Lebens und des Creutzes an uns kam, auch so gleich mit demselbigen Hoffnungs-Kleid begabet wurden, und ward uns so gleich im heiligen Schauen gegeben, den Tag der völligen Erlösung mit vollen Augen des Geistes einzusehen. Und ob wir wol neben dem in den aller schmertzhafftesten und bittersten Leidens-Proben stunden: so zog uns doch unser Hoffnungs-Kleid immer dort hinein, wo auf den Tag der Erlösung die Krönung mit vollen Freuden folgen wird, welches dann viele Ursachen an die Hand gäb, daß Geister offt angezogen wurden mit Krafft aus der Höhe; also daß wir offt neben unsern unablässigen Leidenschafften in Gleichheit der Englischen und Himmlischen Chören aufgezogen wurden, welches uns nicht allein bey dem freudigen Auf- und Absteigen der Geister nicht konte lassen stille seyn, ohn daß wir nicht hätten sollen in Worten ausbrechen, um die Wunder unsers Gottes zu verherrlichen, sondern wurden so gleich nach Art der Englischen Chören und Thronen Herrschafften und Gewalten angetrieben, den Allmächtigen mit Lieb- und Lobes-Gesängen zu verehren. Und ob zwar wol zu Zeiten die Englischen Chöre ihre Lieder mit uns anstimmeten: so wurden wir doch gewahr, daß unsere Stimmen die wenigste Zeiten mit ihnen ein traffen, wegen der annoch an uns tragenden Grobheit in der noch nicht gäntzlich gereinigten Natur, welches bey uns ein genaues Aufmercken verursachete. Neben dem allem verliesen unsere unablässige Leidenschafften uns nicht, sondern wurden

(✝✝)

Vorrede

den. mehr gehäuffet, weilen wir eine Untüchtigkeit bey uns spüreten, daß
wir GOtt nicht konten, nach dem vollen Eindruck des Geistes verherrlichen.. Wiewol wir erkennen, daß die Natur nicht ganz unter dem Creuz
aufgerieben und vernichtet sondern unter demselben geheiliget und in eine
Englische Klarheit aufgelöset müßte werden. Neben dem dachten wir: ist
unsere Natur nicht einmal bequäm einen deutlichen Thon zu einem Englischen Gesang von sich zu geben: wie wollen wir dann tüchtig seyn zu wich-
tigern und höheren Dingen, nemlich wo man GOtt im Geist ohn Unterlaß
Tag und Nacht dienet in seinem heiligen Tempel. Daneben sollen unsere Leiber und Geister seyn Tempel und Wohnungen des heiligen Geistes:
dann der heilige Geist nicht wohnet in einem unreinen Gefäse, sondern
nur in saubern Geistern Hertzen und Naturen.
Dieses hat uns Ursach gegeben GOtt auch von ausen auf die aller-
sauberste Weise zu dienen: weilen wir wusten, daß Er keinen Gefäl-
len an dem Geplärr der Böcke und Geschrey der wilden Tiere; aber wol
an dem Lob seiner Heiligen hat. Und weilen wir dann merckten, daß der
Geist des Singens so gar säuberlich will bedienet seyn: so gab
es uns mehr Ursach mit demselben in Freundschafft uns einzulassen, als zu
gedencken, daß etwas bey der Sach zu verlieren wäre, wie wir es auch erfäh-
ren. Dann so bald wir uns einliesen: so fanden wir nicht allein keine
Ursach zur leichtsinnigen Freude und Lust, sondern wurden so gleich mit
der allerbittersten und wehmütigsten Leidenschafft beladen, daß
auch unsere gantze Menschheit daran gecreutziget war. Und weilen man
nichts gesinnet war, denen Leidenschafften aus dem Wege zu gehen; sondern
blieb stehen, und hielt an am Werck: so ists geschehen, daß unsere gantze Menschheit nach eben demselben Grad der Leiden in eine
gewisse Geschlacht-machung und Dünnheit gebracht/ wodurch
allerdings der reine und saubere Geist der Göttlichen Weißheit, als der ein
Meister dieser hohen und Göttlichen Kunst ist, eine offene Thür gefunden,
und uns nach allen und jeden Graden der Leiden diese Englische Sing-
Kunst aufgesiegelt, welches sich endlich so weit ausgebreitet, daß allerdings weder Maas noch Ziel mehr darinnen zu finden war. Wes wegen man auch genöthiget war, dieses hoch theure Geschenck nicht für sich allein zu behalten, sondern auch anderen Liebhabern des Göttlichen und Himmlischen

Ueber die Sing-Arbeit.

lischen Lustspiels mit zu begünstigen, und die Sach so an Tag zu legen, wie sie gegeben, und unter viel Gedult und Langmuth nacheinander auf gesiegelt. Und ob wir auch solten von denen Meistern und Künstlern der irdischen und unteren Weißheit getadelt werden, weilen wir annoch mit dieser unserer edlen Gabe in diesem untern Theil der Welt zur Herberge sind, und doch nicht nach derselben Gleichheit mit unsrer hohen Gabe auftreten: so vergeringert solches unsern edlen Schatz nicht allein nicht, sondern bewahret uns mit demselben, daß sich nicht etwas Fremdes allzu sehr in uns verliebe. Dann so wir mit dieser hohen Gabe nicht anderst erscheinen könten als nach Art der Künstler dieser sichtbaren Welt-Weißheit: so wäre ja kein Unterscheid zu sehen, ob diese unsere Sach von unten her, oder ob sie von oben her, ob sie aus dieser Welt, oder von jener Welt Weißheit entstanden; doch wollen wir uns nicht länger mit dieser Sach aufhalten; sondern weiter fortfahren. Und wiewol wir allerdings mit dieser unserer Vorstellung am End sind: so ist uns doch das nöthigste und nützlichste noch übrig, worinnen beschrieben soll werden, was zu allererst nöthig bey einem recht artigen Lehr-Meister zu observiren bey denen anfahenden Lehr-Jüngern dieser hohen Kunst, und was hernach die Sach in ihrem Wesen und Adel seye, wann nemlich bey der Sach geblieben, und sie nicht mit fremder Materie vermenget wird. Hernach soll auch selbst denen geübten Schülern in unserer Schul ein gründlicher Bericht von dem Geheimnuß der gantzen Sache ertheilet werden: wie zu erst alle Arten der Melodien in sich selbst ihre eigene Manier und Art haben; wie und auf was Weise die andern Stimmen zu passen, und was vor Buchstaben auf eine jede Weise nach ihrer Art eintreffen, daß sie nicht dißharmoniren, und einander entgegen lauffen. Und das wollen wir ihm so wie gegeben.

Der Himmel, der sich schon vor langen Zeiten auf uns hernieder gelassen, bleibe auf uns beruhen mit der Heiligen Taube die bishero unsere Vorsteherin und Rathgeberin gewesen in allen unsern Wegen, daß sie uns dann unter viel Gedult und Leidenschafft kein Geheimnuß der Liebe unsers Gottes verhelet, sondern die Pforten der heimlichen und verborgenen Weißheit aufgesiegelt, und zu uns heraus getreten, uns in Vorblick das Geheimnuß des Paradieses geöffnet, und so gleich

(††2.)

Vorrede

im H. Schauen uns angereitzet/ um mit dergleichen Sachen beschäfftigt zu seyn/ welche alldorten in jener Welt werden vorkommen/ von dem reden wir.

WANN wir solten beschreiben den Nutzen/ so wir bey Gelegenheit dieser Sache erfahren: so solten wir uns wol ins Unendliche ausbreiten müssen/ weilen wir in Erfindung dieser hohen Gabe gar ungemeine hohe Studien erlernet. Da wir dann nicht allein unsern Gewinn aus dem Nutzen der Sache selbst holeten: sondern wurden daneben des gantzen Menschen Abfall von GOtt kundig/ wie nemlich demselben so gar nichts Cörperliches über geblieben von dem wahren Guten/ oder auch nur eine blinde Gestalt, daß nur ein Bild könte von dem wahren Wesen dargestellet werden; sondern ein pures und lediges Nichts-seyn, das weder Gestalt noch Farben von etwas Wahrhafftiges darzustellen vermag, welches alles uns sehr klein und gering in unsern eigenen Augen machte. Dabey wir also demnach in diesen unsern Schulen mehr Erfahrungen erlernet, als zuvor in vielen und langjährigen Leidens- und Glaubens-Wegen, weilen uns diese hohe Schule allen unsern Ghaben Reichthum und Schönheit hinweg nahm, also daß wir nun zum voraus gar kühnlich sagen dörffen, wie auch allerdings nöthig zu wissen, sonderlich in Ansehung dieser hohen Göttlichen Gabe und Schule, daß wir gefunden, welches wir allerdings wollen an die Spitze gestellt haben; wie daß nemlich kein einiger Mensch von Adam u. Eva geboren vermöge einen deütlichen Thon von sich zu geben/ der in dieser Schule zu passen wäre/ noch weniger einen rechtartigen Gesang helffen zu zieren. Wobey sich am meisten zu verwundern, daß sich der Fehl des Thons allemal darinnen findet/ nemlich daß er die rechtartige Höhe nicht erreichet/ die in dem Gesang dieser hohen Kunst vorkommt/ woraus zu mercken, daß der natürliche Mensch von unten her u. von der Erden, diese hohe Kunst aber von oben her und vom Himmel. Dahero auch das beständige Stricken

Ueber die Sing-Arbeit.

cken und Fallen im Singen vorkommt, da in allen Umständen niema-
len sich einiger Fehl zeiget, der im hohen Auffsteigen über den recht-
tigen Thon vorkommt, welches wir alles in vielem und wichtigem Nach-
dencken beherziget, was nemlich der abgefallene Mensch seye, und wie un-
tüchtig er sey zu Göttlichen Sachen, weswegen wir allerdings an diesem
Ort wollen den Anfang machen, weil solches zu allererst vorkommt. Doch
ehe wir weiter schreiten, wollen wir einen Schritt zurück gehen, und zu
erst noch ein wenig betrachten, was neben dem allem zu dieser hohen
Kunst gehöre, dieweil unser Sinn nicht darauf aus ist, dieser hohen Gabe
der von GOtt hoch-gradirten Sing-Kunst viel Schmuck und Ehre in
Worten anzulegen, weilen sie schon zuvor alles dessen voll, und genugsam
ist, sich selber anzupreisen. Darum wir uns auch nicht viel mit dergleichen
Sachen wollen aufhalten, sondern zur Sach selbst schreiten; doch ein We-
niges im Vorbeygehen melden, welches dieses hohen Geistes Art und
Wesen seye, und durch was Mittel wir uns bey Ihm können beliebt machen, daß wir in seine Gleichheit kommen.

Die Weißheit von oben/ die bishero unsere geheime Rath-
geberin/ Führerin und h. Unterricht gewesen in allen unsern
Wegen/ und uns dieses hochtheure Geschenck entsiegelt und
aufgelöset; die gebe fernerhin einem jeglichen/ daß er in seinem
Thun GOtt gefällig und den Menschen werth/ so wird sich
auch wol die Gabe/ so zu dieser Kunst gehöret/ mit finden.

Ob zwar wol bey vielen Unwissenden viele unbedächtliche Urtheile gefället
werden, gleich als ob man mit dieser von GOtt hochgeadelten und gradir-
ten Kunst mit dem Geiste dieser Welt in Gleichheit stünde; so könne wir doch
solches ganz und gar nicht gestehen; sondern vielmehr das Gegentheil zu
erweisen haben, weilen wir zu dieser wichtigen Sache weder fremde Farben
noch grause Haar gebraucht; sondern blieben alleine bey den menschlichen
Stimmen, als die durch das Bewegen der Herzen und Geister angetrieben zu Lob und Ehre dem Allmächtigen. Denn so die geheime und
verborgene Weißheit nicht wäre zu uns heraus aus ihrer Kammer getreten; es solte uns wol diese Göttliche Kunst ein geheimes Räzel und ver-
siegelter Brief geblieben seyn. Sintemal wir gestehen schlechter dings dem
Geist dieser Welt keine Kunst zu, die zum Gebrauch himmlischer Dinge nö-

thig

Vorrede.

thig; fondern wir legen vielmehr ihren Urstand dem Paradies bey; aber doch fa, daß es in denselben erstorben, wie auch der Mensch am Himmelreich erstorben, und doch, wann er durch den rechten Geist erwecket wird, wieder tüchtig wird ins Himmelreich einzugehen. Also ist auch in dieser Sache zu verstehen, wenn sie durch den rechten Geist erwecket wird.: so gehet sie wieder mit ins Paradies ein, weilen daselbst ihr rechter Urstand und Heimat ist.

WATERMARK OF THE ZIONITIC BROTHERHOOD, IN THE TWO FIRST PARTS OF THE TURTEL TAUBE, SIG. A TO M, PP. I TO 90.

These were evidently pri▒▒▒ several years prior to date on the title page. The continuation is printed upo▒ ▒▒▒what lighter paper. Two editions of the Turtel Taube were printed, one for ▒▒▒ ▒▒▒se, 5¾ × 7⅜ inches; the other one, on larger and much heavier paper, 6½ ×▒▒▒▒, for church use. The copy of the latter in the writer's collection also bear▒ ▒he water▒mark 1744.

CHAPTER VII.

LET us now proceed directly to the subject, and show, as briefly as possible, by what means and opportunities we may, both spiritually and physically, attain to this art of high degree, and then consider further whatsoever things the circumstances of the case may require. In the first place, be it observed, that divine virtue must be viewed from the summit of perfection, and occupy the first place, if one would become the right kind of pupil and thereafter a master of this exalted and divine art.

"Furthermore, both pupil and master ought to know how necessary it is, in addition to all other circumstances, to embrace every opportunity to make oneself agreeable and acceptable to the spirit of this exalted and divine virtue, inasmuch as according to our experience and knowledge it has within itself the purest and chastest spirit of eternal and celestial virginity.

"This naturally requires compliance with the demands

of an angelic and heavenly life. Care must be taken of the body, and its requirements reduced to a minimum, so that the voice may become angelic, heavenly, pure and clear, and not rough and harsh through the use of coarse food, and therefore unfit to produce the proper quality of tone, but on the contrary, in place of genuine song, only an unseemly grunting and gasping.

" At the same time it is especially necessary to know what kinds of food will make the spirit teachable, and the voice flexible and clear ; as also what kinds make it coarse, dull, lazy and heavy. For it is certain that all meat dishes, by whatever name known, quite discommode us, and bring no small injury to the pilgrim on his way to the silent beyond. Then there are those other articles of food which we improperly derive from animals, *e. g.*, *milk*, which causes heaviness and uneasiness ; *cheese,* which produces heat and begets desire for other and forbidden things ; *butter*, which makes indolent and dull, and satiates to such an extent that one no longer feels the need of singing or praying ; *eggs*, which arouse numerous capricious cravings ; *honey*, which brings bright eyes and a cheerful spirit, but not a clear voice.

" Of bread and cooked dishes none are better for producing cheerfulness of disposition and buoyancy of spirit than *wheat* and after this *buckwheat*, which, though externally different, have the same virtues in their uses, whether used in bread or in cooked dishes.

" As regards the other common vegetables, none are more useful than the ordinary *potato*, the *beet*, and other *tubers*. *Beans* are too heavy, satiate too much, and are liable to arouse impure desires. Above all must it be remembered that the spirit of this exalted art, because it is a pure, chaste and virtuous spirit, suffers no unclean, pol-

luted and sinful love for woman, which so inflames and
agitates the blood of the young as completely to undo
them in mind, heart, voice and soul; whilst in the more
mature it awakens excessive desire after the dark things
of this world, and consequently closes heart, mind and
voice to this pure spirit as its haven.

"As concerns *drink*, it has long been settled that nothing is better than pure, clear water, just as it comes from
the well, or as made into soup to which a little bread is
added. Every other manner of cooking, however, whereby
the water is deprived of its healthgiving properties and
turned into an unnatural sort of delicacy, is to be considered as a vain and sinful abuse; just as other articles
of diet, which we do not deem worthy of mention in this
place, have, through many and diverse lusts, been turned
from their natural and harmless use into delicacies. Of
those who gormandize we cannot here speak, for we are
concerned only with those who are already engaged in the
spiritual warfare, and who in all respects strive lawfully.
With those who walk disorderly and unlawfully we,
therefore, have nothing to do. It of course stands to reason that the power to exercise divine virtue is not to be
sought in the selection of this or that particular diet; for,
were this the case, we would wish, if it were possible, to
be entirely relieved of eating, so that we might lead an
Enochian, supernatural and supersensual life. Then this
heavenly wonder-song would of itself break forth, without
the addition of any of those things that are only transient
and never reach eternity.

"And now, not to dwell upon this matter too long, let
us take up the next part of our subject. Let us first say,
however, that if we were to undertake as complete an ex-
position as the subject demands, we would fail to reach the

end. Nevertheless, we will spare no pains to make it as clear as possible; but, let it be borne in mind that we will still leave something for the educated and practical (musician) to study and think over."

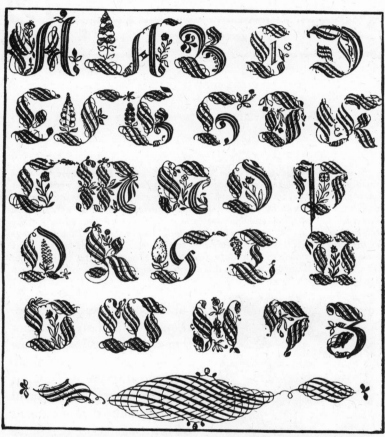

ALPHABET USED IN THE MANUSCRIPT TUNE BOOKS OF THE EPHRATA COMMUNITY.

Die Sing=Arbeit.

CHAPTER VIII.

BEISSEL'S DISSERTATION ON HARMONY.

Translation by the Rev. J. F. Ohl, Mus. D.

TRANSLATOR'S NOTE.

It will be evident to any musician who reads this "Dissertation," or who examines any of Beissel's compositions, that beyond the most rudimentary knowledge of the common chord and its inversions, he had little understanding of the laws of harmony, and none whatever of meter and rhythm. The work done by him and his associates is therefore correspondingly crude and inaccurate, and it becomes interesting only from the fact that it belongs to the first attempts made on American soil to compose sacred music. The translator has aimed to reproduce the evident thought of the writer rather than his exact language, which is often very obscure, and most difficult to render into idiomatic English.

HE all-important and most useful qualification in a teacher of new pupils is first to know that he must not teach them merely to sing the A, B, C, or the seven letters, and then at once introduce them to thirds and intervals before they have learned the characteristics of each letter, or, indeed, understand what they have learned. Special care must be taken to bring out the distinguishing quality of each letter (*i. e.*, note or sound); and this requires such diligence and costs so much labor that we cannot here describe it. The voices may either be harsh and unsympathetic, or false notes, that do not reach the required pitch, may be sung. In such cases efforts must not be relaxed until it is learned and seen how much remains to be overcome; but if one seems to be totally incapable, let him desist for a time, in order that he may not become entirely discouraged.

"When the characteristic quality of each letter (note) has been taught, diligent efforts must be made to train the voice; and such directions must be given regarding tone-production as will enable the singer himself to correct mistakes. For at this stage of the instruction everything that is needed for ultimate success may be imparted, whilst at the same time so much may be overlooked as thereafter to require years to make good the loss.

"And now let us proceed to show what constitutes a four-part tune, and what letters (notes) in the other parts must accompany the melody in the different keys; then also to give a diagram of the keys, and to indicate how the pitch may be raised when it has fallen.

"Let it be known that not more than three letters (notes) can be used for the four parts. Consequently the fourth part is always the octave. The three letters (notes), however, always appear at the beginning of each tune. Thus we obtain the four parts. The three letters (notes) which appear at the beginning must be regarded as the masters and lords that dominate everything from beginning to end, inasmuch as the tune must close with the same letters (notes) with which it began.

"If the melody is in the key of C, E is the note in the

Ueber die Sing-Arbeit.

bis man mercket und siehet, wie weit es einer dem Düncken nach zubringen
hat. Scheinet etwa eine gäntzliche Unfähigkeit zu seyn, so gebe man es eine Zeitlang mit solchem auf, damit man sein Gemüt nicht gar verstürtzt ma-
che. Wann aber eines jeden Buchstabens Art heraus gebracht ist: so muß
hernach aller Fleiß angewandt werden, daß man die Stimme lerne brechen,
und was eines jeden Buchstabens Art seye, anweise, auf daß er sie lerne verstehen, damit, wann hernach soll weiter gegangen werden, man sich bey Feh-
lern und Mißschlägen zu helffen wisse. Dann es kan allerdings an diesem
Platz alles geholet werden, was hernach in der gantzen Sache nöthig, und
kan auch so viel versehen werden, daß es hernach kaum in viel Jahr kan her-
um geholet werden. Das ist nun dieses: Nun werden wir an diesem Pfo-
sten nicht weiter gehen, sondern wollen den graden Weg darlegen, was einen 4. Stimmigen Gesang ausmachet, und was bey allen und jeden Wei-
sen nach ihrer Art vor Buchstaben in einer jeden Stimm auf den Choral passen, wie auch den Schlüssel einer jeden Weiß in 4. Stimmen auf einer Ta-
sel sehen lassen, und wann ein Gesang gefallen, wie er wieder zu he-
ben, daß er nicht auser seiner Art und Manier gesetzt werde.
    Es ist zu wissen, daß nicht mehr als 3. Buchstaben seyn können, so die
4. Stimmen ausmachen, weswegen die 4te Stimm allemal mit der Octav
geschieden wird, welche 3. Buchstaben dann allemal bey einer jeden Melo-
die gleich von Anfang aufgetreten kommen, daß sie uns die 4. Stimmen geben, wobey dann zu mercken, daß diese 3. Buchstaben, die im Anfang vor-
kommen, die Meister und Herrn sind, wo alles von Anfang bis zu Ende muß
auf beruhen bleiben, weilen der Gesang allemal am End wieder mit eben denselben 3. Buchstaben aushalten muß, womit er angefangen. Ist es eine
C-Weiß, so ist und folget sein Anderer, als der e. und machet den Schlüssel zu dem * Barrir, der g. ist sein Dritter, da dann der obere den Tœner, u.
der untere Choral g. den Baß anfängt; doch kans kommen, daß sie verwech-
selt werden, wenn nemlich der Choral nicht just mit dem C. anfänge, doch
bleiben sie beysammen, fangen den Choral an, und endigen ihn auch. Was
noch sonsten die anderen 4. Buchstaben, die wir hier Knechte nennen, an-
langt, als f. a. h. d. so soll einem jeden von selbigen sein Mitknecht bemercket
werden, wie sie nemlich zusamen stimmen. Und ob wir zwar wol am Ende alles auf Tafeln wollen sehen lassen, so wollen wir doch daneben den Fleiß
                                              (†††)   thun

* Der Barrir ist nach der gemeinen Redens-Art der Tenor, der Tœner aber der Alt.

Barrir[1] (tenor), and G in the *Toener* (alto). Thus the alto and the bass begin on G. This order may, however, be inverted, when, *e. g.*, the melody does not begin with C. Nevertheless these letters (notes) must remain together and begin and end the tune.

"As regards the four remaining letters (notes), F, A, B, D, which we shall designate servants, let each be told how he must serve his fellow-servants, so that they may harmonize. And although we shall show all this in diagrams at the close, we will now give ourselves the additional trouble' of explaining which must be the two associates of each of these letters (notes).

"If F occurs in the melody it is served by D in the tenor and bass, and by A in the alto; A demands D in the tenor and bass, and A in the alto, sometimes also in the bass; B calls for D in the tenor, and G in the alto and bass; D asks for B in the tenor, and G in the alto and bass. In this manner a melody in C may be harmonized in four parts.

"Let us now show how the pitch may be recovered when it has fallen. To do so, the beginning must always be made with the key-note. If the melody is in C, sing C, D, D♯; then call D♯ C, and continue on this pitch.

"Now let us proceed from the key of C to the key of A (minor). Here again let us first give attention to the three masters with which the four parts must begin and

---

[1] Conrad Beissel here gives an explanatory footnote regarding the use of the terms *Barrir* and *Toener*, stating that in ordinary language the former stands for tenor, the latter for alto. Both of these terms were used arbitrarily by Beissel, as neither appears to have been known to the Rev. H. Ernst Muhlenberg, the best philologist in Pennsylvania during the last quarter of the eighteenth century. In a previous translation I was misled in the use of these terms by a person to whom I submitted my copy under the impression that he was an expert musician. In the present translation the modern terms are used wherever they occur.—JULIUS F. SACHSE.

end, and then bring together the four servants and assign each his duty. As A is here the ruler (key-note) of the melody, its associates are C in the tenor (occasionally also in the bass), and E in the alto and bass. This is the four-part chord in the key of A (minor). The remaining four servants which do duty besides, are F, G, B and D. F calls for B in the tenor, and for D in the alto and bass; G

Four-part Key for Melodies in C.

for E in the tenor and bass, and C in alto; B for G♯ in the
tenor, and E in the alto and bass; D for B in the tenor,
and G in the alto and bass.   If the pitch has sunk I must
call the C I am singing A, ascend to a new C, call that
A, and continue.   Thus we also clearly see how to bring
melodies in A (minor) into four-part harmony, and how to
regain the pitch when it has fallen.

" Let us now pass from melodies in the key of A (minor)
to those in the key of B♭.   In the latter key B♭, D and F
are the lords and masters.   B♭ is the key-note of the
melody, D governs the tenor, and F the alto and bass,
though B♭ indeed remains the ruler in the bass.   The
four servants are G, A, C and E♭.   Of these we associate
G with the melody, but C with the tenor and bass (though
the upper G more conveniently takes E♭ in the bass),
whilst the alto invariably becomes E♭.   A calls for C in
the tenor, and F in the alto and bass; C for A in the tenor,
and F in the alto and bass; E♭ for C in the tenor and
base, and G in the alto.   If the pitch has fallen I call my
B♭ G, ascend the proper number of degrees to a new B♭,
and sing on.

"And now let us look at these melodies in which G is
the ruler, and B♭ and D are the associates (G minor).   In
these we come to a wonderfully strange turn, inasmuch
as altogether different letters (notes) are made to do service in the three other parts.   We begin with the three
masters.   In these melodies the parts start with G, B♭
and D.   Let it be understood that the three letters (notes),
invariably stay together and form the beginning of a tune
in four parts; that, as already stated, the fourth part is
the octave; and that it does not matter with which of these
three letters (notes) a tune begins.   That in our description we always begin with the letter which designates the

(1) C MAJOR, (2) A MINOR, (3) G MINOR, (4) G MAJOR.

KEY DIAGRAM FROM THE SCORE BOOK OF THE CLOISTER.

(5) B♭ MAJOR, (6) F MAJOR, (7) E♭ MAJOR, (8) C MINOR.
KEY DIAGRAM FROM THE SCORE BOOK OF THE CLOISTER.

key in which the melody is written, is done for the sake of
accuracy. This is also the reason why, in our account,
we seem to insinuate that all melodies begin with the
letter (note) which is the chief in the melody (the key-
note); yet this is not possible. In our further description
we will, therefore, continue to be governed by the special
characteristics of the melody. This, then, is the manner
of those melodies in G that contain B♭ (G minor). G in
the melody takes B♭ in the tenor, and D in the alto and
bass. This is the chord, and it remains the same through
the whole piece, excepting that when G is sustained in
the melody, the tenor always sings B instead of B♭. This
is also the case with melodies in A (minor), in which the
tenor sings C♯ to a sustained A in the melody. The four
remaining letters (notes) F, A, C and D♯ (E♭), serve as
follows: F requires B♭ in the tenor and bass, and D in
the alto; A demands D in the alto and bass, and F♯ in
the tenor; C calls for A in the tenor, and for F in the alto
and bass; and D♯ (E♭) is served by G in·the tenor, and by
E (probably meant for C—Tr.), in the alto and bass. To
raise the pitch when it has sunk, proceed as under melodies in B♭.

"We now come to the melodies in G that have B and
F♯ (G major), in which G, B and D form the triad and
give us the four parts. The remaining letters (notes) F♯,
A, C and E are treated as follows: F♯ is served by B in
the tenor (sometimes also in the bass), and by D in the alto
and bass; A by D in the tenor and bass, and by F♯ in the
alto; C by upper E in the tenor, and by A in the alto and
bass; E by C in the tenor and bass, and by A in the alto.
The directions given under melodies in B♭ will show how
the pitch may be raised.

"There yet remain the melodies in F, in which the triad

F, A, C gives us the four parts. The remaining four servants G, B♭, D and E are disposed as follows: G is served by C in the tenor and bass, and by E in the alto; B♭ by D in the tenor, and by G in the alto and bass; D by B♭ in the tenor and bass, and by G in the alto; E by C in the tenor and bass, and by A, sometimes by G, in the alto. If the pitch has fallen, I do as indicated above, *i. e.*, I get another F by singing F, G, A♭, and then calling A♭ F, on which pitch I continue.

"We have now imparted, as well as we are able, the secret of our spiritual song. Although in this work (the *Turtel Taube*) we are more concerned with hymns than with tunes, and a well-informed person might ask why so much has been said about music when none appears in the book, we have yet thought it proper to write this introduction, partly because from music the hymns in this volume derive their attire and adornment, and partly because it will stimulate lovers of this noble and paradisiacal art to inquire further into its secrets."

Thus ends Beissel's extraordinary Dissertation on Harmony, which was the basis of the Ephrata music. A few short paragraphs of an apologetic character conclude his "*Vorrede über die Sing-Arbeit.*"

FACSIMILE OF WATERMARK IN WRITER'S LARGE PAPER COPY OF THE TURTEL TAUBE ; *vide* pp. 65 *supra.*

CHAPTER IX.

Original and Modern Notation.

N conclusion we present a few examples of Ephrata music, in their original form as well as in modern notation. One of the most characteristic of these is *Die Braut ist Erwachet*, set in four parts. How the original score of this tune was written on a single staff is shown on the following page.

It will be noticed that all this music is very strange in its progressions, and violates almost every rule of harmony, as is to be expected from one who was not an educated musician. This fact, however, does not lessen the historic value of these unique compositions, but rather tends to increase our admiration for the enthusiastic celibates of the mystic community on the Cocalico, who, at so early a day, in the midst of their primitive surroundings, found time and inspiration to work out their own system of harmony and compose so many original hymns and tunes.

The rendition of this music was as peculiar as the music itself, and was sung according to the old records in a falsetto voice without opening wide the lips. The result, we are told, was a " soft measured cadence of sweet harmony." The true Ephrata vocal music virtually died out with the community.

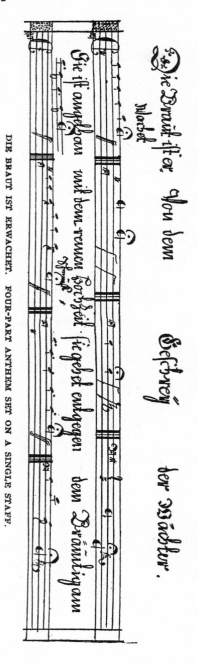

DIE BRAUT IST ERWACHET. FOUR-PART ANTHEM SET ON A SINGLE STAFF.

MUSIC AS WRITTEN FOR AND USED BY THE SECULAR CONGREGATION.

"DIE BRAUT IST ERWACHET," AS AN ANTHEM FROM MS. HYMN AND TUNE-BOOK.

ANTHEM DIE BRAUT IST ERWACHET TRANSPOSED INTO MODERN NOTATION.

After the singing schools became established, the celibates, male and female, were divided into five choirs, with five persons to each choir, namely, one soprano, one tenor, one alto and two bass singers. The sisters were divided into three choirs, the upper, middle and lower; and in the choruses a sign was made for each choir, when to be silent and when to join in the singing. These three choirs had their separate seats at the table of the sisters during love feasts, the upper choir at the upper end, the middle at the middle, and the lower at the lower end. In singing antiphonally, therefore, the singing went alternately up and down the table. Not only had each choir to observe its time when to join in, but, because there were solos in

AN ANTHEM ARRANGED TO BE SUNG ANTIPHONALLY FROM WUN-
DERSPIEL, p. 9.

ARRANGED AS A HYMN FOR FIVE-PART CHOIR. TURTEL TAUBE, HYMN 13, PART ONE, p. 66. ZIONITISCHER ROSENGARTEN, p. 27.

NO. 98, PART FOUR, pp. 402, TURTEL TAUBE.

ZIONITISCHER ROSENGARTEN, p. 102.

each chorale, every voice knew when to keep silent, all of which was most attentively observed.

The next illustration presented here is the hymn *Wohl-auf wohl-auf und schmück dich.* This is also given in both the original and the modern form. Both of the above melodies, with that of the seven-part choral *Gott ein Herrscher aller Heiden* were artistically rendered by Mrs. Frank Binnix at our annual gathering at Harrisburg, October, 1901.

An illustration of the five-part setting " *Wie ist doch der Herr so gütig*," is given upon the previous page.

The words and music of this hymn are by Sister Anastasia (Anna Thomen), who afterwards eloped with and married Johannes Wüster, the Philadelphia merchant.

How the same words and tune were frequently set as an anthem as well as a hymn is shown by the two versions of the hymn *Gott wir kommen Dir entgegen*, on pages 84 and 85.

An illustration of music set in six parts is also presented in the original form. This is taken from the *Paradisches Wunderspiel*, or the great choral book of 1754.

In closing our paper upon the music of the cloister we present a version of the celebrated seven-part motet *Gott ein Hersher aller Heiden* transposed into modern notation. The same criticisms as to progressions that apply to the other pieces apply also to this composition.

Gedencke, HErr, an David und sein Leyden, weil er die selbst geschworen hat, daß er Dir dienen will zu allen Zeiten

AN EPHRATA MOTET IN SIX PARTS. TURTEL TAUBE, HYMN 27, P. 192. PARADISCHES WUNDERSPIEL, HYMN 100, P. 71. CHORAL BOOK, P. 195. WEYRAUCHS HUEGEL, HYMN 20, P. 71.

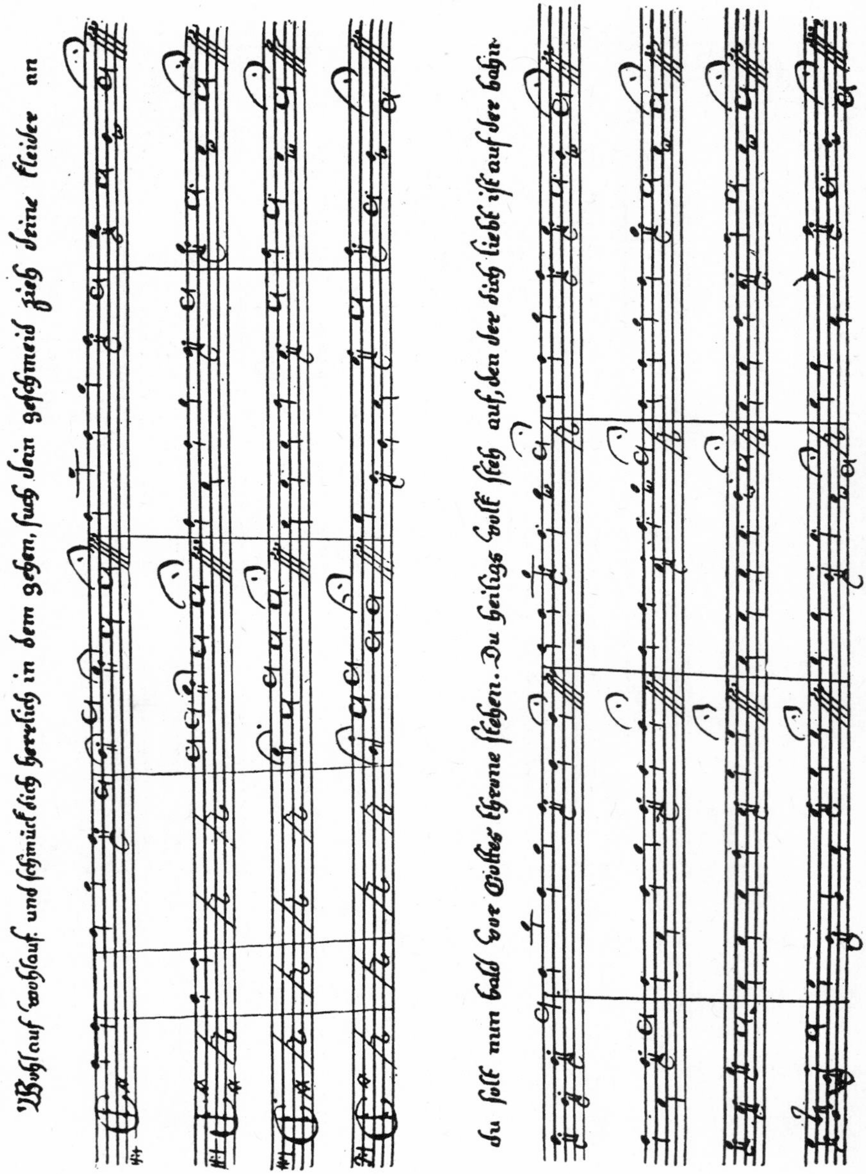

FROM MS. TUNE AND HYMN BOOK.

WOHLAUF, WOHLAUF, UND SCHMÜCK DICH HERRLICH.

Wohl-auf, u. schmück dich herr- lich in dem Geh - en, such dein Ge-schmeid, zieh dei- ne Klei - der an; wohl-auf,

du sollst nun bald vor Got - tes Thro - ne ste - hen. Du heil- igs Volk steh auf, denn der dich liebt ist auf der Bahn.

AS TRANSPOSED INTO MODERN NOTATION.

GOTT EIN HERRSCHER ALLER HEIDEN.

SEVEN PART MOTET. WEYRAUCHS HUEGEL, HYMN 652, p. 740. TURTEL TAUBE, HYMN 30, p. 196. WUNDERSPIEL,
HYMN 108, p. 75. ZIONITISCHER ROSENGARTEN, p. 51.

SYMBOL AND MOTTO OF THE EPHRATA COMMUNITY.

Appendix.

A Page of Ephrata Theosophy.

READ AT THE ANNUAL MEETING OF THE PENNSYLVANIA
GERMAN SOCIETY, EPHRATA, PENNA.,
OCTOBER 20, 1899.

By
JULIUS FRIEDRICH SACHSE, LITT.D.

LANCASTER, PA
1903.

Kurz gefaßte.

Nützliches

Schul = Büchlein

Die kinder zu unterrichten, in Buchstabieren,
Lesen, und auswendig lernen,

Deme angehänget ein kurzer doch deutlicher, und
gründlicher

Unterricht
Zur Rechenkunst.

Aufgesetzt zum Nutz und Gebrauch vor Kinder.

Von L. H

Zweyte Auflage.

EPHRATA.

Gedruckt und zu bekommen bey dem Schulmeister,
Drucker und Buchbinder 1786

TITLE PAGE OF HOECKER'S EPHRATA PRIMER.

EPHRATA THEOSOPHY.

AMONG a mass of papers and manuscripts which it was the good fortune of the writer to examine some months ago, dating from the provincial period, and relating more or less to the upper end of Lancaster County, there was one that particularly attracted his attention.

This was an old manuscript, yellow and discolored by age. It was written on the ordinary coarse writing-paper, such as was the product of the paper-mills on the Wissahickon and Cocalico. The writing was still distinct and clear, done in a firm hand, with a well-pointed quill, showing that the writer must have been one of education and experience.

Upon the outside, as a legend, it bore the old German proverb or *Sprüchwort:*

"Quäle nie ein Thier aus scherz,
Dann es fühlt wie du den schmerz."

("Ne'er torment a beast in sport,
For it feels like you when hurt.")

Upon examining the paper it proved to be a plea for mercy toward the brute creation. This ended with an earnest entreaty for social purity, and incidentally illustrated the theory of the migration of the soul.

The more it was examined, the greater became the interest in the subject and the manner wherein it was presented. The only possible clue to authorship was the endorsement upon the first page : " Obed, *ein wallender nach der seligen ewigkeit.*" This was the signature and Kloster name of Ludwig Höcker, one of the most devout members of the Ephrata Community, who was the schoolmaster of the settlement, and has the honor of having established, in 1739, the first Sunday-school of which we have any record. Brother Obed was also one of the instructors in the classical school or academy maintained by the Brotherhood, and the present paper is evidently one of his lectures or discourses delivered before the higher class. He was a prominent character in the Ephrata Community, and a firm supporter of Prior Jaebez.

When he was in his seventieth year, and the institution was already verging into a state of decline, the old philosopher published a second edition of his primer and schoolbook.

Upon the reverse of the title he gives as a reason for its publication that " if it be used by the children, it will prevent, in every case, the destruction of a Psalter or a Testament "; thus showing that the chief text-book of the Ephrata system of education was based upon the daily use of these two fundamental parts of Holy Writ. At the

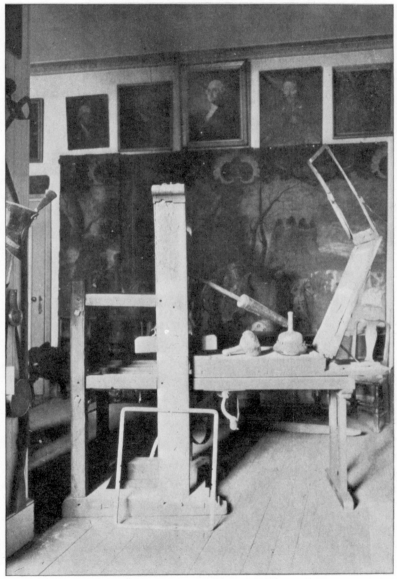

J. F. SACHSE, PHOTO.

ONE OF THE EPHRATA PRINTING PRESSES.

IN COLLECTION OF HISTORICAL SOCIETY OF PENNSYLVANIA.

time of its issue, as will be seen from the title, the pious
recluse then filled the position of schoolmaster, printer and
bookbinder to the Brotherhood. Brother Obed died during the summer of 1792, after passing the allotted three-
score years and ten.

The paper under consideration has the distinction of
being the earliest effort made in this country to prevent
cruelty to animals, and to inculcate in the minds of the
growing generation the duty of protecting and respecting
the virtue of the gentler sex. The illustrations in the
course of the lecture are occasionally of a somewhat har-
rowing nature; at the same time, we must bear in mind
the state of the country and its people at that period, when
it will be found that the similes are well suited to the times
in which they are used.

It matters but little whether or not good Brother Obed
was the author of the paper. There were others among
the solitary recluses equally devout. At the same time it
is an excellent illustration of the code of morals taught in
this community. Then, again, we have here the earliest
known plea for the two movements which now, in the closing years of the nineteenth century, have become a fashion-
able fad. It is but another illustration of how the Pennsylvania German has lost the honor and credit due to him
through his innate modesty.

Here the lecturer was far ahead of his time. What
fruits his labors bore, both history and tradition have failed
to record. What great good was accomplished by this
plea, so quaintly and forcibly presented to the youth of the
middle of the eighteenth century, will never be known.
Even the existence of this essay was unknown and forgot-
ten until it fortunately fell into the hands of the writer, and
is now translated into the language of the country :

Geiſtliche

Briefe

eines

Friedſamen

Pilgers,

Welche er von 1721. bis an ſeine 1768.
darauf erfolgte Entbindung
geſchrieben.

———————————

Ephrata, gedruckt im Jah 1794.

Title page of a unique Ephrata Imprint in the collection of the writer.

 HILE sitting in my chair and dozing one evening, it seemed to me that I heard a voice saying: "Take up your pen and write what I dictate." I looked around whence the voice came, but could see nothing. My lamp was still burning, but the room was empty. I was alone. Then I felt that it was my guardian spirit (*Schutzgeist*) who had made his presence known, so I at once prepared myself to write, when the voice dictated the following story:

" I was the oldest son of a country gentleman, who was possessed of large wealth, and when I was about nineteen years of age, I was thrown by my horse while hunting, and by the fall dislocated my neck, and from a lack of immediate attention, died before I could be taken home.

"In the next moment, to my inexpressible sorrow and surprise, I found myself in the shape of a pug-dog, in the stable of a country tavern kept by a man who formerly had been my father's butler, and married the cook. As a pug, I really received many caresses. Alas! my master, to increase, as he said, my beauty and strength, soon afterwards cropped my ears and cut off a piece of my tail. In addition to the pain this operation caused me, I quickly experienced in a thousand ways what great inconvenience this mutilation subjected me to, and how it placed me at disadvantage. At the same time, this was but the least part of my misfortunes, which I was destined to suffer in this condition.

"My master had a son who was about five years old, and

even more of a favorite than I was; and as his whims and passions were condoned as soon as they manifested themselves, he was encouraged to vent his spite against any living or inanimate thing which offended him, by beating me. When he did any damage (of other transgression no notice was taken) the father, the mother, or servants were ever ready to flog me in his place.

"This intercourse with persons whom formerly I had but looked at with disdain, and was wont haughtily to command, was not to be endured; so, early one morning, I ran away. Although it was raining hard I kept on my journey until the afternoon without intermission. It was about four o'clock when I came to a village, and at a house where some carpenters were at work I noticed a heap of shavings under a temporary cover to keep them dry. So I crawled, as I believed, unnoticed into a corner and lay down. Alas! a man, who was just working on some lumber, seeing that I was a strange dog and of the pug variety, conceived the idea of amusing himself and his fellow-workmen at my expense. For this purpose he bored a hole about two inches in diameter in a piece of deal. He then caught me suddenly and poked the stump of my tail through this hellish machine, and with a hammer drove a heavy wedge beside it, so as to firmly fasten all together. The act crushed the bones and cause me indescribable torture. As he set me down, the wretches who witnessed this barbaric play, broke out into boisterous laughter over the painful efforts to which I gave expression, in my miserable attempts to escape and release myself from the board which I was forced to drag after me. They hissed me until I was out of their sight. In the meantime, as fright, pain and embarrassment urged me on with an unwilling speed, I ran with such force between two posts,

which were not far enough apart to let my block pass
through, that the board with the remains of my tail stayed
behind. Soon after, I found myself on the grounds of a
gentleman farmer, where I saw in the distance the large
watch-dog ; so, fearing to be torn to pieces, I continued in
my flight. Alas! several farmers at work in a barn some
distance off, seeing that I ran without being pursued, that
my eyes gleamed, and that I was frothing at the mouth,
imagined I was mad and struck me dead with a threshing
flail.

" Thereby I was released from this mutilated and perse-
cuted body, and found myself under the wings of a flicker,
together with three others just hatched. I now rejoiced in
the thought that I, like my mother, would be a denizen of
the air, and could swing myself aloft to such a height that
no human cruelty could reach me. Alas! even before I
could rightly fly, my mother was surprised in her nest by
a school-boy, and in her attempt to escape was squeezed
so hard that soon after she died. The boy thereupon took
the nest, and all there was in it, and placed it in a basket
where I soon lost my three companions in misery by the
unsuitable food and improper attention. I remained alive,
and after I was able to feed myself, my tyrant's mother
took me as a present for the daughter of her landlord.
This young girl was a beautiful creature, in her eighteenth
year.

" My imprisonment now seemed to lose its terrors. I did
not have to fear the rough fist of an ignorant lout whose
caresses were even more to be dreaded than his anger,
who, even in his passion and inclination for a new toy, was
apt to neglect me and let me starve to death, or would
twist my neck for the penny given him to buy my food.
I now became accustomed to confinement in a cage ; I was

hung out of a cheerful window, and regularly fed by one of the most beautiful hands in the world. Thus I fondly imagined that henceforth, being under the shelter of the tender caresses of this fair being, with every evidence of love and affection, no sorrow would come to me.

"My fate, however, was destined otherwise. As a young lady from the city made an afternoon call at my mistress' house, the latter embraced the opportunity to exhibit me with others of her pets, among which were a parrot, a monkey, and a small dog. She whistled and held out her finger; I hopped upon it; she stroked my feathers, and I laid my head against her cheek, and, further to show my appreciation and how I valued her attentions, I began to sing. As soon as my lay was ended, the visitor turned to my mistress and said that the dear creature would necessarily become the most beautiful singing bird in the world if its eyes were burned out, and it were confined in a narrow cage.

"This dreadful suggestion was sanctioned by my beautiful mistress, upon the repeated assurance that my song would be greatly increased thereby. Accordingly, upon the next day, she undertook the inhuman operation, according to the given directions, using the point of a heated knitting-needle.

"My condition may now be easier imagined than described. Fortunately I was not permitted to endure the sad loneliness of constant darkness for any extended time, as on one occasion, in the dusk of the evening, a cat came unnoticed into the room, pulled me through the bars of my cage and ate me up.

"I was far from dissatisfied to be again released from both blindness and imprisonment, and in the shape of a May-bug to fly about in the air. However, I had scarcely entered into this sphere of my existence when a gentleman, in whose garden I was seeking food on a cherry leaf, caught me and gave me to his son, a little fellow who was just luxuriating in his first pair of trousers, saying: 'Here, Charlie, is a bird for you.' The boy received me with pleasure, expressing Satanic joy, and forthwith impaled me alive, as he had been taught, upon a needle fastened to a linen thread. Thus I was condemned to afford pleasure to my young master by sailing around in the anguish and torment of death. When I was completely exhausted and unable to use my wings any longer, he was told to crush me under foot, as I was of no further use, a command which he executed in a merciful manner by scrunching me in an instant in the dust.

"From a May-bug I migrated into a rain-worm, and found myself esconced in the dung-heap of a farm-yard. By this change of my condition I consoled myself with the reflection that, while I could not now rise in the air and with the rapidity of thought take myself from one place to another, I was at least in a position where I could neither be a pleasure to mankind nor evoke their enmity, both of which had proven equally disastrous to me. Thus I hoped now to end my life in peace, as in my humble condition I would escape the notice of the most cruel of all created creatures.

"Alas! I was not suffered to rest long in my fancied security. One morning I was disturbed by an unusual noise, and remarked that the whole earth around me trembled. Quickly crawling up to the surface to learn the cause, I no sooner got to the top than I was eagerly seized by the person who had loosened the earth with a digging-fork for just the purpose of what had brought me to the light. Thus, together with many others of my kind, all companions in misfortune, I was thrown promiscuously into a broken pot, and soon after became the property of a tender-hearted shepherd who found his pleasure in angling.

"The next morning this man took us to the banks of a stream, and forthwith took out one of my companions; and, while whistling a lively tune, forced a barbed fish-hook through the entire length of the worm, as the point entered at the head and emerged at the tail. The unfortunate animal squirmed on the bloody hook in pain and suffered torture greater than any human being ever experienced, and which no animal can feel whose muscular vitality does not extend to all parts of its being.

"In this condition it was thrown into the water as bait for a fish, until it, together with the concealed hook, was swallowed by an eel. As I witnessed this tragedy I made my own reflections upon the great disproportion between the pleasure of catching the game and the torment inflicted upon the bait. However, these reflections were suddenly dispelled by the identical anguish of death of which I had just been a witness.

"You would not have space enough upon your paper if I were to relate to you all that I suffered from the thoughtless brutality of the human race: what I experienced as a cock, a lobster, and a pig. It will suffice to say that I have suffered equal to the malefactor who is broken on the wheel, for I was boiled alive upon a slow fire, and beaten to death with five thongs, to tickle the sensual palate of the epicure or furnish enjoyment for the rabble."

Thus far I had been the amanuensis of an unseen mentor. During the continuation of my musing I felt something tickle my hand. As I lifted my eyes from the paper to see what it was, I found it to be a common house-fly, which I immediately caught and killed by holding it in the flame of my lamp. In an instant the fly disappeared and a young maiden of exquisite form and beauty, in all the glory of budding womanhood, stood before me. "Thoughtless wretch," said she, "you have once again changed the condition of my existence, and have now exposed me to far greater fatalities than any to which I have thus far been subjected. As a house-fly, I was your mentor and I might have escaped from your cruelty, were it not my intention to instruct you. Alas! now it is impossible for me to remain concealed, and therefore equally impossible to be safe. The eyes of sensuality and unbridled desire are centered upon me. Man will henceforth use all his wit, and employ an indefatigable resolution to lead me into dishonor and vice. But, although man still remains my enemy, and henceforth attacks me with greater ardor and persists in his desires with greater stubbornness, I have now less strength to withstand him than formerly. There is an element within my own bosom which will exert itself to annihilate me; its influence is constant, and a constant influence is not easily overcome. In the meantime publish unto the world what I have disclosed unto you; and if perchance thereby a single human being is turned from the exercise of a guilty inadvertence to do aught for the protection of the inferior creatures, and also by these considerations to prevent the unfortunate results of one's inhuman actions, which cause pain and suffering, then I have not suffered in vain.

"But as I am now exposed to accidental as well as to incidental evil, and as I not only stand in danger of wanton caprice and indiscretion, but also of the wicked designs of cunning and knavery, therefore, in order to expiate for some of the great wrong you have done me, let it henceforth be your bounden duty to warn, in public print and upon all proper occasions, the female sex against the snares that are laid for their destruction, and discourage the male sex from all attempts to decoy and debauch innocence. Show unto the latter the enormity of their crime, which they heap upon themselves, and picture to them the shameless, dissimulating treachery that they commit under the guise of ardent and tender affection for that beauty and innocence alone which makes love credulous, and in its guilelessness is free from suspicion, and is thus cast into unfathomable misery."

As I listened to this charge, my heart beat so strongly that the anxious efforts I made to answer awakened me.

INDEX.

Alphabet, script, 29.

Anastasia sister, 86.

Apology for sacred song, 23, 24.

Arndt's prayers, 17, 21.

Ausbund geistlicher Lieder, 43.

Barrir and Toener, Beissel's explanation of, 72-73; note on, 73.

Beans, Effect on voice, 67.

Beissel, Conrad, theories, 13; Wunderschrift, 18; English version, 19, 21; dissertation on harmony, 22, 50, 71-79; apology for sacred song, 23-24; as composer, 23, 28; hymns by, 49; instructions on the voice, 66-69.

Billings, William, 11.

Binnix, Mrs. Frank, renders music, 86.

Blum, Ludwig, 29.

Braut des Lamms, 45.

Braut Schmuck, Geistlicher, 45.

Buckwheat, effect on voice, 67.

Butter, effect on voice, 67.

Cheese, effect on voice, 67.

Chronicon Ephratense, 13; title, 20.

Cloister, music of, 27.

Dissertation on harmony, 70-79.

Dissertation on man's fall, 19, 21.

Drink, effect on voice, 68.

Early Christians, song of, 25.

Eggs, effect on voice, 67.

Ephrata, pen work, 12; sampler, 14; brother house, 14; sister house, 15; cloister history, 15, 17; unique imprints, 17, 21; score book, 23; sister, 32; watermark, 65; script alphabet, 69; symbol, 92; theosophy, 95-106; primer, 1786, 94; a new imprint, 98.

Fahnestock, Dr. Wm., portrait, 16; mention of, 17.

Geistlich briefe, title, 98.

Geistlich Denckmahl, 48.

Geistliche Lieder, ausbund, 43.

German sectarians, mention of, 17; error in, corrected, 22, 23, 52.

Gott ein Herscher aller Heiden, 29; original score, 30.

Harmony, Beissel's, 14.

Hertzen's Bewegung, 1749, 44.

Historians, soi-disant, 16.

Höcker, Ludwig (Bro. Obed), primer, 94; mention of, 96, 97.

Honey, effect on voice, 67.

Hymnals of Ephrata Community, 33; title pages of, 1730, 34; 1732, 35; 1734, 36; 1736, 37; 1739, 38; 1747, 39; 1754, 40; 1755, 41; 1756, ib.; 1762, ib.; 1766, 42; 1785, 43.

Jaebez, Prior, 22; portrait of, 51; mention of, 52, 96.

Key diagram from score book, 76, 77.

Leben eines Herzogs, 21.

Marshall, Christopher, 22.

Melodies, in C, four part, 74.

Miller, Rev. Peter — vide Jaebez Prior.

Milk, effect on voice, 67.

Morgen-Röthe, Abend-ländische, 46.

Movable C clef, 29.

Music, earliest Ephrata, 10; at Snowhill, 11, 12; MSS., 13; unlike reformation tunes, 14; how sung, 15; score book, 22, 23; four-part music on single staff, 23; new material, 27; alleged portrait, 28; movable C clef, 29; arrangement of voices, 29; seven-part *ib.* on single staff, 81; four-part key, 74; key diagram, 77; on single staff, 81; double staff *ib.*, Die braut ist erwachet — original and modern, 82, 83; four-part anthem, 84; same in five-part, 85; six-part setting, 87; wohlauf, wohlauf, original and modern four-part, 88, 89; seven-part motet, modern notation, 90, 91.

New England psalm singer, 11.

Notation, original and modern, 80.

Nunnery, Snowhill, 11.

Obed, Bro., see Höcker, Ludwig

Ohl, Rev. J. F., Mus. D., 27; note by, 70; translation by, 70–79.

Paradisisches Wunderspiel, 29; title, 42.

Peculiar rendition of music, 80.

Rosen und Lilien, title of, 41.

Reformation music, 14.

Sacred song, Beissel's apology for, 23.

Score book MS., Ephrata, 23.

Score, four-part on single staff, 81.

Sectarians, German, 17.

Seidensticker, Prof. Oswald, 17.

Singing school of kloster, 84; classes in, 84.

Sister, sketch of, 32.

Snowhill nunnery, 11, 12.

Theosophy, Ephrata, a page of, 93–106.

Transmigration of the soul, 99–106.

Thomen, Anna, 86.

Tubers, effect on voice, 67.

Turtel Taube, 13, 22, 23; title page of, 39; Nachklang, 41; neuvermehrtes, its sub-titles, 44, 45, 46, 47, 48; various editions, 47; epilogue, 50; Neuer Nachklang, 52; foreword, 53–58; facsimile of prologue, 59–65; water-mark in, 65, 79; dissertation on harmony, 70–79; Kirren, von, 45.

Voice, Beissel's instructions on, 67; milk, effect on, *ib.*, cheese, *ib.*, butter, eggs, honey, wheat, buckwheat, effect on, *ib.*, drink, effect, on, 68.

Voices, peculiar arrangements of, 29.

Wheat, effect on voice, 67.

Wunderschrift, Beissel's, 21.

Zerfallenen, Hütte Davids, 47, 48.

Zionitischer Rosen Garten, 49.

Zionitic watermark, 65.